D1187827

University of Ulster
LIBRARY, PORTRUSH

009152581

STANDARD LOAN
Return or renew by the date below
Fines will apply to items returned

The Library is operated by
UU Bibliotech Ltd, a wholly
owned subsidiary company
of the University of Ulster

Human Relations For The Hospitality Industry

WITHDRAWN FROM THE LIBRARY OF UNIVERSITY OF ULSTER

Human Relations For The Hospitality Industry

Robert J. Martin
Associate Professor
College of Hotel Administration
University of Nevada, Las Vegas

and

Donald E. Lundberg
Dean, School of Hospitality Management
United States International University

 VAN NOSTRAND REINHOLD
New York

Copyright © 1991 by Van Nostrand Reinhold

ISBN 0-442-00676-4

All rights reserved. No part of this work covered by the copyright hereon may be reproduced or used in any form by any means — graphic, electronic, or mechanical, including photocopying, recording, taping, or information storage and retrieval systems — without written permission of the publisher.

Printed in the United States of America.

Van Nostrand Reinhold
115 Fifth Avenue
New York, New York 10003

Chapman and Hall
2-6 Boundary Row
London, SE1 8HN, England

Thomas Nelson Australia
102 Dodds Street
South Melbourne 3205
Victoria, Australia

Nelson Canada
1120 Birchmount Road
Scarborough, Ontario MIK 5G4, Canada

16 15 14 13 12 11 10 9 8 7 6 5 4 3 2 1

ACKNOWLEDGEMENTS

According to Dr. Lundberg, the original concept for Part I comes from Clarence Hedlenbrand's *Front Office Psychology* published in the early 1940s. Other individuals who have generously contributed ideas and criticism to Part I of the book include Professors Jeffery Wachtel and Arthur Hanson, Bruce Epstein, Hugh Harper and Hermina G. Mendez, Guest Relations Manager for Hotel Inter-Continental, San Diego.

My thanks to them all.

Parts II and III draw heavily on the front line employee application of Transactional Analysis concepts, and on current participative management and situational management theories.

PREFACE

After all is said and done, human relations in the hospitality business goes back to what Elsworth Statler, founder of Statler Hotels, said: "Life is Service." Human relations involves the never-ending search for more effective interpersonal relations, concern for the other person's well-being, awareness of that person's frame of mind, state of fatigue and psychological needs at the moment. Hospitality "servers" of all ranks and levels have chosen to serve the public and, within limits, to please the public. Knowing what to say, how and when to say it and when to be quiet has always been a highly prized skill — one that smoothes human relations, avoids unnecessary tension and friction between people and adds to the pleasure of living. Social facilitation expedites business transactions.

The newly-arrived guest walks in the door and face-to-face guest relations begin.

Guest's impressions about and toward the hotel set in, and many of those impressions are formed by the person behind the desk. Guest relations (relations between guests and employees) are initiated and may continue throughout the guest's stay. How the person behind the desk looks and feels, what is said or not said, the body language expressed, all color the guest's feelings about the hotel and the hotel experience. The guest's expectations also bear on perception, so that what is pleasant and reassuring in a bed-and-breakfast home may not be so in a high-style resort or a luxury hotel.

The employee involved in guest relations must not only be proficient but must also be intuitive as to the guest's perceptions.

This book is divided into three parts. Much of the first part is based on experience and common sense. Part II presents an analytical tool, transactional analysis, that can be useful in human relations. Part III deals with employee relations (the interrelation between managers and staff at all levels as they will ultimately bear on guest relations).

TABLE OF CONTENTS

PART I
GUEST RELATIONS

Chapter 2 (continued)

Chapter 4 (continued)

PART II
TRANSACTIONAL ANALYSIS
An Analytical Tool for Guest Relations

Chapter 8 (continued)

PART III- EMPLOYEE RELATIONS
The Basis of Quality Guest Relations

PART I

GUEST RELATIONS

INTRODUCTION

The hospitality industry is recognized as the most labor-intensive industry of our time, but one which is tolerant of entry-level work-skill requirements. Because entry-level positions require only moderate skills and time to train is not extensive, most positions are paid at or near the minimum wage. There are, however, more than adequate opportunities for employees to advance.

Many skills are required in our industry, but the more important skills are those which relate to how we treat our guests. Additionally, it is not management that has intensive contact with our guests, but our front-line employees. The purpose for being in the jobs we hold has roots in the question our employees continually ask our guests, "May I be of service?" And the quality and manner in which that question is asked and executed by our front-line employees is vital. This quality, however, does not originate at the entry-level position, but at the top of our organizations. We must, therefore, conclude that it is the inspired treatment (leadership) of our employees emanating from above that filters down through the organization (as employee relations) which sets the stage for the kind of treatment to which our guests will fall heir. For this reason, it is vital that managers and supervisors, at all levels, learn how to deal with their employees fairly, with respect and in a way which will encourage participation in quality and concerned service to our guests.

Because of the competitiveness of our industry, those properties which fail to put quality and concern in their guest service training are doomed in the future to see their customers enter the restaurants and hotels across the street. For this reason, every employee must become involved, to whatever degree possible, in keeping guests wanting to return for future visits to our hotels and restaurants.

Along with initial skills training, the development of service personnel must be vigorously continued in the areas of organizational development and human relations. With a demand for labor that grows daily, coupled with a shrinking labor force, we must ask ourselves, "How do we meet our staffing requirements of the future?" Best we inspire *the employees we currently have* to stay with us and be a part of our team.

CHAPTER 1

THE HOSPITALITY BUSINESS AND GUEST RELATIONS

The term "guest relations" implies that the customers are given the same welcome, warmth and concern for their well-being as though they were guests received in the privacy of a home. A major commodity in the hospitality business is hospitality, i.e., the cordial reception and treatment of guests that makes the guests feel wanted, appreciated and secure. In the last analysis, hospitality assures guests, our customers, that they are welcome, makes them comfortable, lets them feel better about themselves and ensures their eagerness to return.

Hospitality is important to most service businesses, but especially so in hotels, resorts, restaurants, private clubs and during air travel. Service people are in a "people business," people serving people.

The hospitality business includes cruise ship operation, travel agency operation and also airline sales. Broadly speaking, the hospitality business includes all businesses serving the traveling public, and may even include auto services, gift-shop services and grocery stores selling to the traveler. This book concentrates on guest relations in hotels and restaurants. Guests in restaurants are traditionally called customers or patrons; we will call them customers rather than guests.

Realistically, the term "guest relations" is partly euphemistic. Hospitality businesses, after all, are businesses, and businesses must be profitable to remain in business. Guest relations, in most cases, cannot be the same as hospitality in the home. In a 1000-room hotel, it is more difficult to convey the feeling of hospitality than in a 50-seat restaurant or a bed-and-breakfast accommodation. No matter what size the operation, guest relations is an ongoing effort to please guests and make them feel more pleased with themselves — and to do so at a profit.

Guest Relations Employees

Who are "guest relations" employees? Broadly speaking, they are all the people who work in the hospitality service industry: those who sell the services, take the reservations, greet the guest on arrival, register, escort, seat and serve the guest; they are the front-line employees, the guest-contact employees, the unseen people behind the scenes who make the end-product service possible. They are the cooks, the baggage handlers, the maintenance personnel, the room attendants, maintenance personnel, custodial people, the night porter and the dishwashers. On the front line are the telephone operators, the reservationists and the receptionists. Many luxury hotels employ personable individuals who are titled Guest Relations personnel — often very attractive ladies and gentlemen who concentrate on making the hotel guests feel welcome, wanted and "very important." Many hotels follow the tradition found in luxury European hotels providing concierge service — employees who, in addition to the front desk personnel, attend to special guest needs such as arranging travel, theater tickets, sightseeing tours or dinner reservations.

A good example of the type of person who is successful in this business is the person who can simply say, "Good evening," but convey an entire concept, like, "Welcome! We're glad you're here with us. We want you to be comfortable and enjoy yourself while you're here because we genuinely care and are concerned about you. And, if everything isn't just perfect, we want you to let us know immediately so we can correct

4

the problem and make it right. We are more than just courteous; we are concerned, and there is a difference. You may feel it while you are with us. And, when you leave, we want you to remember us and come back again and again."

Guest Relations personnel do not have to be in front of the public all the time to convey their feelings to the guest. Many employees are behind the scenes but recognize why they are in their jobs. Their attitudes are conveyed to the guest by how they act toward their co-workers that do have contact with the guests. They have sparkle in their tone and demeanor. They join in at appropriate times to give an "at home" feeling to the guest, but are careful not to impose or interrupt unless absolutely necessary.

For example, the room attendant who is asked directions by a guest in the hotel hallway does not have to say, "Wait, I'll call a manager." Room attendants do not have to say, "I don't know," either, because the answers to such questions have been a part of their training.

The Hospitality Persona

The thrust of this book is the meaning and practice of service: service without servility, loss of dignity or loss of integrity. It is not a Pollyannaish attitude of blind optimism. American service should be neither obsequious nor demeaning, favoring neither fawning nor kowtowing. Such behavior toward the vast majority of Americans makes them uncomfortable or embarrassed. Straightforward, friendly, helpful service is usually expected, service with few overtones of class difference.

The service offered differs somewhat according to price. A person staying on the club floor of a luxury hotel expects a concierge who may speak several languages and who is knowledgeable about restaurants, etc. The same person traveling cross-country may stop at a budget motel where the front desk is staffed by a pleasant local. The service is "good," as expected in both places. The club floor carries a $200 a night tariff; the budget motel costs $30. A posh hotel may invite the guest to be seated at a mahogany desk to register, then an assistant manager in a cutaway coat may escort him or her to the room, followed by a bellperson carrying the luggage. At a budget motel where the guest is a regular, the registration may consist of, "Hi, Charley, how are the kids?" The reception and service offered are appropriate to the situation.

"Good" service varies from culture to culture. Swiss hoteliers are businesslike, highly efficient and somewhat impersonal; service is fast; accommodations are spotless. South Koreans offer deferential service, with constant attention to guests' wishes. Passengers flying Korean Air are greeted on the plane by a group of bowing flight attendants. Flight personnel devote themselves to the wishes of the passengers. In contrast, service aboard Aeroflot, the Russian national carrier, is completely impersonal and consists largely of instructions issued by the flight attendants.

Guest relations can be simple or complex. They always involve feelings — good feelings of mutual satisfaction and gratitude, bad feelings of annoyance, resentment or indifference. Many of these feelings, good or bad, result from the human relations skills and the attitudes of the server.

Guest Relations: Serving another. Meeting others' needs. "What's in it for me?" one asks. Plenty. Aside from helping the hotel or restaurant prosper, good guest relations can be exciting work which makes life a lot easier, giving employees more job control. Smoothing relations with guests, such as defusing potential guest problems can be very exciting and gratifying work. Perhaps more importantly, good guest relations produces pride.

Note that the word "serve" is used through this book. Nearly everyone, no matter what rank or fortune, serves in one way or another and is concerned with pleasing individuals and/or groups. The politician serves the voter; the physician, the patient; the lawyer, the client; the salesperson, the buyer; the professor, the administrator and the students; the bank

6

teller, the bank patron. Each offers a service to a specific clientele.

Who is a Guest?

We define a guest as:

— A person who deserves the most courteous, concerned and attentive treatment that can be provided.

— Someone to respond to quickly, efficiently and with sensitivity.

Why do guests favor one establishment over competitors?

— A good product, food and lodging plus some pleasant feelings.

— Courteous treatment.

— Attentiveness to needs.

Feelings count. A good feeling can come from getting a bargain, more for one's money. For others, the good feeling results from being seen at some "special" place having a prestigious address.

The product; the room, the meal, the ambience of the facilities are enhanced by courtesy, attentiveness, responsiveness, effort and concern. Care is a good word to remember because it can remind one of several key attributes. For example:

C   Concern

A   Attentiveness

R   Responsiveness

E   Effort

The long-range goal of guest relations is to provide room, food, beverage and entertainment to the guest and in so doing, achieve a financially successful operation with due regard for the people who provide such services. Product, price and convenience may be competitive. Guest relations can be the critical advantage. The way a guest is treated, what staff say and do, the way they say it, creates positive or negative feelings toward the hotel or restaurant. For the guest, the service staff is the business.

The Professional Persona

For those guest-contract persons who feel that it is insincere or phony to act friendly when they do not feel friendly, how about being "professionally friendly"?

Professionals define and place limits on their relationships with guests. They play a role, the role of a professional.

In the plays of ancient Greece, the actor went on stage with a mask depicting the emotions of the person he was to portray: happy, mirthful, fearful, in pain and so on. Everyone, when slipping into the job role, assumes a mask, i.e., the kind of "persona" called for on the job. We all go through life trying to play the roles called for, that of a father, a mother, a teacher, an officer, a diplomat.

The guest-contact employee also roleplays. The role calls for being well-ordered, calm, responsive and responsible. The employee steps into the role the moment work begins.

Behavior and Real Feelings

Behavior analysts say that, if one continues to act in a certain way, the actions themselves may influence the real feelings. Continuing to smile even though one does not feel joyful, expressing solicitude while feeling little of it, acting positively when feeling otherwise, influences the person to begin feeling what the actions portray. Conversely, acting negatively creates negativism in the actor.

The conclusion: Act courteously even when not feeling courteous. Behavior which is perceived as courteous may direct the hospitality employee's behavior toward real feelings of helpfulness and consideration.

Know Thy Guests

Philosophers and spiritual leaders say, "Know Thyself." That saying could be changed to "Know Thy Guests." Where do they come from? How did they get here? Why are they here? And what do they expect of this hotel or restaurant? Satisfaction is largely a matter of expectation. Expectations when eating in a fast-food restaurant may be minimal and certainly different than expectations when dining in a luxury restaurant. Expectations for personal service in a hotel that charges $200 a night are considerably different than expectations when the room rate is only $25.

People from the East Coast have different expectations than those from the West Coast. Easterners usually dress more formally (men wear ties more often than in the West where male dress is more casual). As a result, Easterners would expect the staff to be more formally dressed.

Senior citizens may expect some form of deference because of their age, such as not being seated in a draft of air or being assisted to a table due to a physical condition.

Guests arriving after a long flight are almost certainly tired and disoriented to some extent. They may expect this condition to be obvious to the staff, and require a more nurturing form of behavior by a table server.

Wealthy guests who have housekeepers, butlers and household staffs in their employ at home, have expectations built upon being accustomed to personalized service.

Persons used to being in a position of authority have expectations built upon efficiency of operation and are inclined to expect the same type of efficiency in public accommodation service.

Know Fellow Employees

Knowing fellow employees rounds out the body of knowledge required to perform well in guest service positions. Most guest service comes in the form of "team activity", and knowing what you might expect out of a fellow employee under certain circumstances reduces the chance of surprises and makes working together more predictable. Being interested in fellow workers, about where they are from, where they went to school, what their family situation is, knowing what excites them and what they might expect from you is a way of expressing human concern for other employees. This attitude and knowledge helps create an atmosphere and framework wherein teamwork can flourish.

Service Without Servility

In some ways the guest relationship is a business transaction. There is a buyer (the guest) and a seller (the hospitality employee). The guest buys attention, concern, courtesy, politeness and a product or service. Deference, yes, but the kind of deference that, traditionally, a gentleman pays a lady, a banker pays a depositor, a younger person pays a senior. Courteous and concerned regard.

There is no loss of respect, only an acknowledgment that the customer is a guest and that the employee is ready and eager to be of service. Courtesy and concern pays and is paid for. Consider the following example:

Mary, a room clerk, is concluding the process of registering Mr. and Mrs. Smith into room 2125. John is a member of the bellstaff and is standing in the position known as "front" which places him next in line to room a guest and, in most cases, earn a gratuity. As Mary completes her routine registration tasks, without looking to see who is in the front position, she simply calls, "Front," and John steps from his post position to the desk, receives the key from Mary to room 2125, and picks up the Smiths' luggage, at which time Mary says to the Smiths, "You will be in Room 2125; the bellperson will show you to your room."

As the Smiths and John depart the front desk area, everything is quietly and efficiently done and there is little if any conversation between John and the guests as they ascend to the 21st floor in the elevator. John knows his place. Upon arriving at the room, John opens the door and invites the Smiths into the room. He quickly places the luggage on the luggage rack, and before leaving the room, expertly says, "Will there be anything else?", to which Mr. Smith replies, "Thank you, no," and hands John $2.00. John says in a most professional manner, "Thank you sir," and departs the room.

Consider the same scene but a different scenario:

As Mary concludes the registration process, she looks up and sees John standing in the front position. She calls, "John," and John steps from the front position to the front desk. Mary then says, "John, this is Mr. and Mrs. Smith from St. Louis. They will be staying in Room 2125." She then turns to the Smiths and says, "John will show you to your room. If there is anything we can do to make your stay more pleasant, please let us know."

As the party starts toward the elevator, John immediately picks up the conversation by saying, "Good evening Mr. and Mrs. Smith. Welcome to our hotel. Have you even been our guests before?" Mr. Smith says, "No, in fact, this is our first time in Chicago." At this point, John quickly tells the Smiths about the hotel and all of its features. He mentions the restaurants and their specialties, then turns to Mrs. Smith and says, "Mrs. Smith, you might be interested in the Mall that connects to the hotel. It is excellent for shopping and all the major department stores are located there. My wife loves window shopping there this time of year." Mrs. Smith replies by saying, "Thank you. Are you familiar with the Museum of Contemporary Art? I look forward to visiting that museum while I am here," to which John replies, "Yes, my wife loves to go to the exhibitions there in the Spring. When I return to the Bell desk, I'll check their hours of operation and phone them back to you." At this time, the party arrives at the room and as John opens the door, he asks, "How was your flight from St. Louis?" to which both Smiths reply that the weather could have been better, that it had been "bumpy." John replies, "I know how you feel. When I have a choice, I'd rather drive and enjoy the scenery." While this light conversation is proceeding, John is turning on the air conditioning and adjusting the drapes for the proper light. He then quickly explains the operation of the TV, message and phone system. He points out the Guest Services Directory on the table, then asks Mr. Smith if he can get them some ice. Mr. Smith says, "No," and John starts to depart the room. Mr. Smith quickly says, "Just a minute, John." At this time, he hands John a gratuity of $5.00 and says, "Thank you for your concern. You have a wonderful hotel here." John says, "Thank you both. We're proud of our hotel. I hope you have a wonderful stay, and if there is anything that any of us can do, please don't hesitate to call any of us. We all thank you for being our guests."

In both scenarios, Mary and John were courteous and efficient, but in the second case, Mary was more friendly and conveyed that a more friendly and family atmosphere prevailed in this hotel. In her manner of addressing John by name and introducing him to the guests, she conveyed that John was not just an automaton but a human being with dignity. John seemed more concerned about his guests and tried to place them in a light and relaxing atmosphere. He was more personable and was proud of his hotel and the team that would be serving the Smiths while they were guests of the hotel.

If John were to be asked why his approach was different, he would probably say, "Because, it is the Smiths and people like them who pay my salary. And salaries are better when you treat people with genuine concern."

Needs Related to Guest Satisfaction

The wellsprings of behavior are needs or drives. Relating customer needs to the diagram below suggests that guest relations can satisfy a range of needs. The diagram summarizes the most popular of motivational theories, proposed by A. H. Maslow[1], a theory that suggests that all humans have a hierarchy of needs and that, at any give time, one or more needs are felt. As the more basic needs are met — those with a physiological basis such as hunger, thirst, sex — other needs, higher in the hierarchy, take over. Once needs for hunger and security are met, social, self-esteem and self-realization needs are activated.

In our society, basic physiological needs for food, shelter and body protection are normally met. Most of our needs are psychic, those for belonging, acceptance and approval by others, and needs for esteem and status. At the top of the hierarchy are the needs for self-realization and self-fulfillment. Psychic needs for recognition seldom are completely met.

A restaurant patron selects a restaurant for its food (physiological needs, level 1); service (esteem and status, level 4); and its atmosphere (needs being met from levels 2 through 5). The server provides food, yes, but more important, psychic rewards.

In Figure 1, the diagram suggests that people go to different kinds of restaurants to satisfy different needs.

A vending machine may satisfy basic physiological needs and time constraints.

Fast-service restaurants satisfy hunger, time constraints, budget constraints and provide a sense of security. They satisfy social needs as well. (For example: The Little League ball team stops by the local pizza parlor after the big game.)

Table-service restaurants and dinner houses offer something more: better food quality, leisurely dining and esteem and status.

Luxury restaurants appeal to those needing peer level approval, ego stroking, and fulfillment, such as the enjoyment of good food and the ambience. Demonstrated deference and interesting foods and wines enclose the person in a cocoon of well-being. The same sort of hierarchy of needs can apply to the selection of a hotel.

Drives Related to Guest Satisfaction

Another motivational theory, this one proposed by Harvard psychologist David McClelland[2], suggests by changing the word "need" to "drive" that behavior can be classified as caused by one of four drives:

Drive for Affiliation

Drive for Security

Drive for Power

Drive for Achievement

A person patronizes restaurants because he or she wants to be with others and to be approved by them (affiliation drive); going to a name restaurant may suggest that a person has "made it" (achievement drive); he or she may go to be seen and respected by other important people (drive for power). Stopping at a luxury hotel can satisfy different drives than registering into a budget hotel.

The FOUR DRIVE Theory and The Veblin Effect

The four-drive theory explains why some people "need" to buy "the best," (drive for achievement) to drive a Mercedes rather than a Ford, to wear Chanel perfume or to live in a million-dollar home.

Some people need prestige; hence the drive for power. Another person may have a need for belonging; hence a drive for security. And the person who must become a member of a certain organization is supporting the drive for affiliation. The reason may be complex or fairly obvious, but the four drives mentioned support different psychological needs.

Staying at a Five Star Resort would not have the status it has if it were sold at a lower price. The buyer wants the distinction of having paid a sizable price, a price that places the buyer among the well-to-do. This has been called the Veblen effect. The Veblen effect can partly account for staying at luxury hotels and eating at expensive restaurants.

MASLOW'S ORDER OR PRIORITY OF HUMAN NEEDS

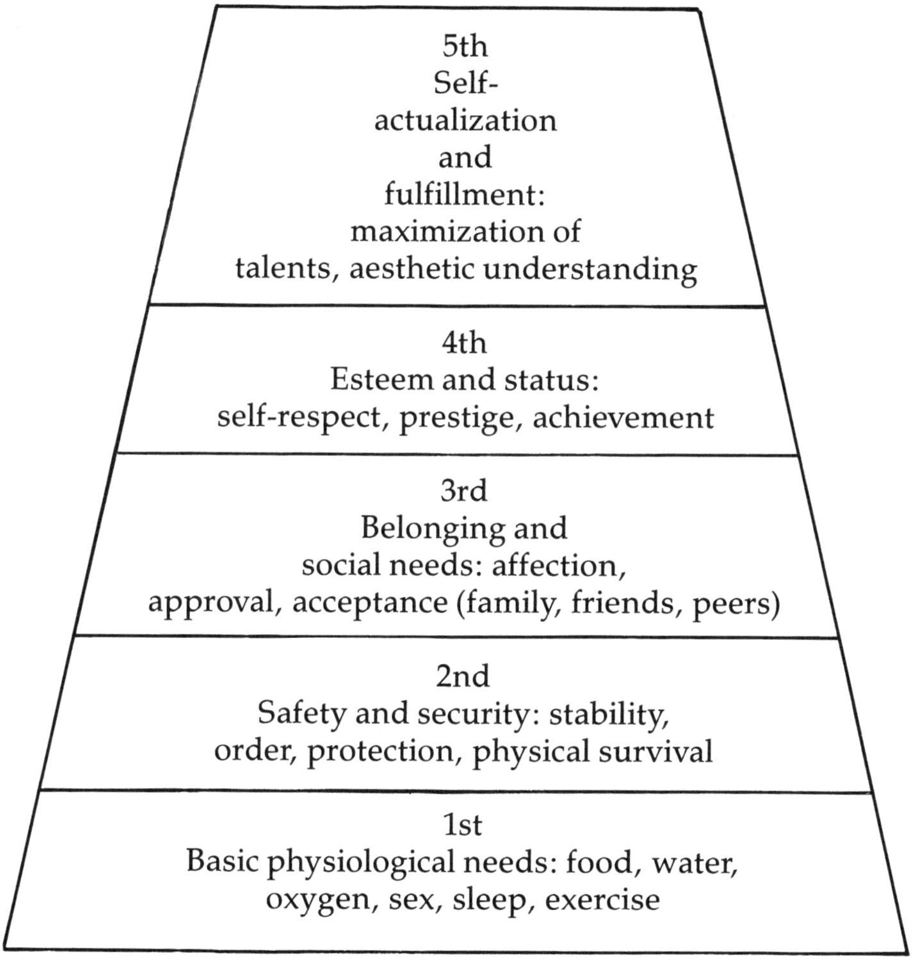

5th
Self-
actualization
and
fulfillment:
maximization of
talents, aesthetic understanding

4th
Esteem and status:
self-respect, prestige, achievement

3rd
Belonging and
social needs: affection,
approval, acceptance (family, friends, peers)

2nd
Safety and security: stability,
order, protection, physical survival

1st
Basic physiological needs: food, water,
oxygen, sex, sleep, exercise

FIGURE 1

Thorstein Veblen, an American sociologist and economist, many years ago described this desire to want to spend more. He called this phenomenon "conspicuous consumption," the practice of buying something which would provide status for the buyer. There may be other reasons for conspicuous buying. People who have been deprived in their younger years often feel relieved to be able to buy something expensive. And there are those who just enjoy spending money. Such people probably get satisfaction out of not having to consider cost as a major factor in a purchase.

Service persons should give these guests more than the normal respect, which is probably what they really want. The buyer expects respect and status.

Without a hereditary aristocracy in this country, many display the accompaniments of wealth by buying fashionable clothing, jewelry, the $1250 suit, the Gucci handbag, by being seen in the celebrity restaurant, vacationing at the expensive resort and by flying or cruising first class.

Courtesy and deference are especially important to such customers.

Rather than attempting to determine which needs and drives are operating in each individual, it is best to assure that each guest is receiving the fullest of attention and concern so that there will be no need to catalog profiles of which guest may be acting under what drive.

Needs and the Guest's Self-Image

Determining what needs predominate in a particular situation may not be easy. People often patronize a particular hotel, restaurant, resort or a particular club because it reflects well on their own self-image. People who think themselves as up-and-comers, or of a certain class, pick places that reinforce the self-image. Harrods of London is a well-known department store catering to the upper classes of England. People who patronize the place do so partly because it enhances their own self-perception.

Self-image may also determine why some people feel uncomfortable in an establishment perceived as higher class. Service personnel may have to be on guard against their own behavior being perceived in any way as putting down the person who is ill-at-ease or on the defensive because of self-image.

The Business Image

Every hotel and restaurant projects an image — good, bad or indifferent. In large part the image is created by guest relations. How the guest is welcomed, treated and served is, using a computer analogy, fed into the customer's computer system. The printout, hopefully: nice place, good service, reliable people.

The guest-contact person provides input data for the customer's computer system. The printout reflects not only the employee's performance but the successful establishment as a whole. In the customer's eyes, the employee represents the business. The image includes employee and establishment.

The intelligent guest-contact employee, aware of the image the establishment is trying to project, strives to create and become a part of the image. Enthusiasm is a particularly pleasing and positive image-builder. Real or otherwise, it reassures the guest, expressing "all is well with the operation" or "should problems arise they can be easily handled."

The Personality Ripple Effect

The effect of a well-groomed, well-mannered, poised guest-contact employee spreads throughout an organization. Employee behavior radiates out and around him or her like ripples caused by a stone tossed into a pond. Enthusiasm or lack thereof, sadness or glee, hostility or goodwill radiate. As has often been said, no one is an island. Feelings and behavior are contagious. The guest is "tuned into" employees, relying upon them for direction and service.

Social Rituals

Most social intercourse is ritualistic. When a person says, "Good morning. How are you today?" he or she is offering a RITUAL STROKE, which is a particular type of POSITIVE STROKE or communication that says, "I'M OK, and I hope you are too. At least, I want you to be OK, like I feel." The answer, "I'm fine, thank you," is a return RITUAL (POSITIVE) STROKE , which communicates a return of the expressed feelings. (More will be said about stroking in PART II.)

Weather comments communicate more feelings than they do fact. Again, "Nice weather we're having, isn't it?" is communicating more of a feeling of well-being than a true and accurate reflection of the weather. This is another example of the RITUAL STROKE. All persons live and depend upon rituals to a certain extent. Rituals take people through the day, provide reassurance and, in the hotel, express a feeling that talking to the person is worthwhile. The ritualistic speaker recognizes the person being spoken to as "somebody" and is concerned enough to say something. Sporting events, and sometimes politics, can be subjects for the ritual. Cynics are apt to put down such rituals as inane, unnecessary or stupid. Far from it. This, too, is social facilitation, smoothing the rough edges of daily life, making guests feel better about themselves and the hospitality business.

ENDNOTES

1. Maslow, A. H., *Motivation of Personality,* (New York), 1954.

2. McClelland, David, *The Achieving Society,* (New York), Princeton D. Nostrand Company, 1961.

CHAPTER 2

THIS MATTER OF COURTESY

Nearly everyone believes in practicing courtesy, at least in principle. But what is courtesy? Actions or words that are well received by others? Is courtesy related to a particular culture and subculture? Will a particular action on one person's part be perceived as courteous by everyone in the same way?

A look at history helps define the meaning of courtesy. Until the time of World War I, courtly manners in the royal domains of Europe were highly formalized. When approaching the Emperor in Hapsburg, Vienna, the courtier bowed three times and did the same when leaving the Imperial presence. Courtesy, although coming from the same word as court and courtly, today means a sincere concern for the other person or, if not sincere, at least a formal relationship, one person responding to another's needs and well-being. Politeness is never ridiculous or out of order.

Good Manners

"Manners", said Ralph Waldo Emerson, "are the happy ways of doing things." Another person put it: Good manners are the traffic rules of a civilized society. Manners facilitate social interaction.

Good manners imply sensitivity to the other person's feelings, avoiding doing or saying anything that unnecessarily offends. It is never good manners to answer a question by a simple declarative "No," even though that is the gist of the reply.

If the employee does not understand what is said, a proper response is "I beg your pardon" or "Would you mind repeating that, Sir?" Never "What?"

Don't tell guests what they must do. "May I suggest . . ." is usually well received.

Courtesy and Manners

Manners, of course, are cultural expressions, and vary from one place to another. The Japanese behave differently than the Chinese. It is acceptable to spit on the floor in a restaurant in China. The Japanese taxi driver is horrified if his white gloves become dusty.

Are manners artificial? Certainly. Do they make social intercourse more civilized? Yes. Do proper manners change over time? Indeed they do. Do manners tend to distinguish between social classes? Yes, especially in places like Great Britain that place emphasis on class distinctions. The problem in America is, just who are those people in faded blue jeans who are reserving the $700 suite?

Are manners in any way related to morals? Not in the least. The cannibal chief was served first. Is our society becoming classless? Not really, but you'd think so the way some people insist on calling everyone by their first names. Better to err on the side of formality than to offend someone by being overly familiar. Does everyone expect or want to be treated equally? Not by a longshot. Why is so much money spent on a Gucci purse when a cheaper one will perform just as well? Why do people buy Mercedes Benz cars or live in huge homes? They want to be looked up to and to be respected.

American class distinctions are made with money - cars, clothes, office appointments. Depending upon the society, status comes with power, position, wealth, lineage and recognized accomplishment.

Our society recognizes a number of merit badges. Travel is

one of them. Where did you stay when in New York? Why the Waldorf; where else? (or any other $300 a night hotel will do.)

"We always fly first class."

Thomas Jefferson, our second president, was an arch proponent of the classless society. We fought the Revolutionary War to rid ourselves of titles and the class system. Right? Wrong! President Jefferson tried to codify his social ideals in the form of a classless etiquette by banning titles and precedence at the White House and public ceremonies. It didn't work. Most of us want to be shown evidence of our worth and we spend lots of money and effort making it possible for others to note our exalted status. The service employee is well aware that much of this concern for status is foolish but goes along with it if only not to hurt the other person's pride.

Judith Martin, a columnist writing under the name of Miss Manners, defends the need for manners and etiquette nicely: "The idea that people can behave naturally, without resorting to an artificial code largely agreed upon by their society, is as silly as the idea that they can communicate by a spoken language without commonly accepted semantic and grammatical rules."[1] Ignorance of the code, she says, is not a sign of virtue. So much for manners and morals.

In the best Korean hotels attractive women bow to everyone entering or leaving the elevators. Restaurant employees line up and bow to departing guests. Flight attendants on Korean and Singapore airlines provide an endless round of smiles and services unknown on U.S. airlines. The Chinese belch following a good meal to show their appreciation for the host's efforts. In Sweden it is poor manners not to bring the hostess flowers or candy. The Japanese bow as an indication of respect. And so it goes.

Manners change. Expressed concern and respect for others is basic in courtesy. Courtesy is a social lubricant serving to define roles, smooth the rough edges of social intercourse, relieve insecurity and create goodwill.

Manners can be an act of vanity or a desire for approval or acceptance. Courtesy is based on thoughtfulness and consideration.

Courtesy and Civility

Courtesy implies warmth and friendliness; civility means the absence of aggression or hostility, forbearance for the actions of others. In other words, one can be civil without being courteous. Obviously there are times when it is almost impossible to muster up any real enthusiasm for a particular guest. The least a hospitality employee can do is be civil, mannerly and go through the motions of politeness.

Courtesy as a Learned Reflex

A professional attitude of courtesy to others is an acquired reflex, learned through practice to the point that it becomes automatic.

While it is true that every individual is unique and each guest different, customer relations are patterned and can be classified. The problem for the employee is to program the self to react to each of the more or less standard guest-relation situations that occur. Once an effective type of response is learned it can be repeated. To be highly skilled in guest relations can be learned.

Here are some examples:

GUEST RELATIONS SITUATIONS & PREPLANNED RESPONSES

1. *Situation:* A guest is waiting in line for seating in a restaurant and asks, "How much longer must we wait?"

   Response: "It will be another five minutes, ma'am. Your table is being made ready at this time. I have selected a nice quiet table for you by the window."

24

2. *Situation:* Table service is slow and the guests are having to wait for service. They have not complained but have had to wait an excessive period of time.

   Response: The table server does not avoid the table but comes to the table and says, "I am sorry you are having to wait. I know how you feel but it will only be a few more minutes. May I refresh your drinks, compliments of the management, while your entree is being prepared?"

3. *Situation:* Guest finds watch missing from personal belongings left in a guest room and complains to the manager that "Someone has taken my watch; what are you going to do about it?"

   Response: "I am sorry your watch has been discovered missing. I will notify our Security and House-keeping Departments at once. They will conduct an immediate search for the watch by looking carefully in your room, and in the laundry through today's soiled linen. If they do not find it, the security officer will make a loss report for our file and will give you a copy in order that you may make a claim against your homeowners insurance."

4. *Situation:* The watch in situation 3 above, is not located by normal search.

   Response: Security officer says, "Sir, our usual search had not revealed the watch. I know how sentimental a watch can be. In the past, guests have inadvertently packed items that were temporarily thought to be missing. Before filing a lost item report, would you please double check your luggage to make sure you didn't accidentally pack the watch away?" Guest checks, finds watch and is now embarrassed. Security officer says, "Please don't be embarrassed; it happened to me one time."

5. *Situation:* Late-arriving guest finds that the hotel has become overbooked and cannot honor his or her guaranteed reservation.

Response: Manager says, "I am sorry but due to a late out-of-order room, I cannot honor your guaranteed reservation. To make amends however, I have made arrangements for you to stay at an equally fine hotel tonight. Our driver will drive you there. In the meantime I will make the necessary arrangements to cover the costs of your first night's room and tax. I will continue to carry your name on our message board in case you get any messages. And tomorrow when you give us a call, I will send a driver and have you returned to our hotel."

Recall that the above responses are preplanned and programmed for specific happenings. Such preplanning helps the self-esteem of the employee and causes the guest to reflect favorably on the employee as caring and action oriented.

Pavlov, the famous Russian scientist, demonstrated how much of what we learn is conditioned reflex. In his experiments, dogs were conditioned to salivate at the presentation of lights or sounds in the same manner as they normally do at the sight of meat. Most animal training today is based on this theory.

People, too, are conditioned to be courteous by being rewarded by parents, peers or teachers. The reward can be a smile or any sign of approval. The moral: If we want employees or those around us to be courteous, reward them immediately when they behave courteously. For example: A Front office supervisor overhears Mary the desk clerk as she handles a guest problem. The supervisor in front of other employees says, "Mary, that was outstanding technique in handling that situation. Your method showed you cared. Keep up the good work."

To extinguish discourteous behavior, ignore it. Over a period of time the behavior, lacking reward, disappears. Courteous behavior, quickly rewarded, takes its place. A climate of courtesy, modeled by management and reflected throughout an establishment, nourishes and reinforces individual behavior patterns of courtesy.

Courtesy as a learned reflex must be practiced following certain guidelines. Take, for example, the "courtesy pledges" that Sheraton employees were asked to make as part of a training program offered in New York City, which follows:[2]

Prepare to like every guest who approaches the desk.

Look the guest in the eye.

Smile with the face.

Smile with the eyes.

Acknowledge each guest in a group by direct eye contact with each one.

Speak clearly but softly.

Stand erectly — don't slouch in front of a guest.

Anticipate the guest's needs.

Wear a watch so you can tell the guest what time it is.

Never tell a guest something will take ten minutes when it will take an hour.

Be specific in giving information or directions.

Shake hands firmly with the guest when appropriate.

Avoid negative expressions like "That's against policy."

Be amiable even when you know the guest is wrong

Help the elderly and the disabled when they need it.

Keep a pen or pencil to lend to guests.

Call guests by their names.

Highlight the benefits of particular guest services such as room movies, fine restaurants, and so on.

Ask the guest if "I can be of help."

Compliment the guest on clothing, hairstyle, if appropriate.

Put yourself in the guest's shoes when he or she has a complaint.

In summary, realize that making the guest feel right *is* right.

Courtesy and Fellow Employees

Accept criticism.

Realize that you can't make others perfect but can work on yourself.

Praise fellow workers.

Develop interdependent relationships with fellow workers so that all perform better.

Laugh and let that laugh influence others.

Never expect respect but always earn it.

Treat fellow workers like professionals; learn that trivia is a large part of everybody's job.

Generate confidence in others by good performance.

Think of the other person first.

General Matters of Courtesy

Give one hundred and ten percent.

Be well groomed.

Think of performing "little extras" in guest service.

Be well read and be able to respond to guests who ask for

up-to-date information.

Contemplate Statler's famous remark: "Life is service."

Face obstacles fairly and squarely.

Be optimistic.

Work at doing the job better every day.

Appreciate that hard work yields happiness.

Start a little early or stay a little late to perfect the job.

Work at showing yourself in order to give more to others.

Concentrate on today — doing the best here and now.

Think back with pride on your courtesy and progress every day.

Admit mistakes and learn from them.

Realize that every day gives the opportunity to learn something new about guest relations.

Be thankful today for the gift of life and the chance to grow.

Practice courtesy — the key to success — until it becomes a habit.

Courtesy is merely concern for the other person, concern expressed in a tactful manner, with respect, attentiveness and a desire to help and to please.

Courtesy and caring go together.

Tact is Always in Order

Avoid phrasing statements or replies in a manner that sounds demanding, uncompromising or dictating.

Word choice can be important. However, much depends on the manner of the reply, whether there is eye contact with the customer, the tone of voice or whether the employee speaks while gazing off into space, mumbles or acts as though the employee is doing the guest a favor in replying at all.

Discourteous Behavior

Some behavior is obviously discourteous. Flirting with other personnel or with guests is in poor taste and often resented by others. Preening, discussing personal problems in view of customers, or any unnecessary conversation can be a form of discourtesy. Slouching, leaning on a table or reading personal mail can be discourteous, as is continuing a personal phone call while a guest is waiting.

Never say to anyone, "You'll have to see the cashier." "You'll have to see the manager." "You'll have to leave your name with the telephone operator." A customer never "has to" do anything, a phrase that puts people on the defensive, in a subordinate position. No one wants to be talked down to, condescended to or patronized. The smart person phrases the same information differently: "Would you check with . . .?" "The credit manager can help you with . . ." "Would you please . . .?"

Front desk receptionists or maitre d'hotels who assume airs and act as though they are aristocrats receiving the homage of their subjects are resented by guests, some of whom become furious. For example: As a resident manager of a large Midwestern resort, this author had the unfortunate pleasure of discussing an unpleasant situation with a young front desk supervisor about how he had handled a problem with a guest. The young supervisor succeeded in only "throwing fuel on the fire." "But I was right, so I was blunt," said the young supervisor; to which I replied, "Is it that important for you to be right? Would you rather be right than have a satisfied guest?" Too often, guests do not complain; they just don't come back.

Eye Contact

Eye contact is of itself a communication that establishes a relationship. Looking directly into the eyes of a person while talking to them is the same as saying, "You have my complete attention and I will not be distracted, nor can I deceive you as

30

long as I am looking into your eyes. My eyes are the windows of my soul and I cannot hide the truth as I know it when I am looking at you, or else you will know it."

When communicating, face the person you are going to talk to and look at him or her. Notice when listening to someone that they immediately begin to lose interest if you do not continue to look directly at them. Eye contact or at least eye-to-face contact feeds the communication process. Don't obviously stare at the speaker but be attentive and give him or her your undivided attention. To do otherwise can be construed as indifference, or even rudeness. Staring, however, can be taken as threatening. Do not look down or look away once you start to speak. These are telltale signs which are interpreted subconsciously by the other person as intimidating, deceitful or threatening.

Eye contact, or lack of it, has overtones of submission or domination, confidence or lack of it. In male-female relations eye contact longer than what is considered proper suggests physical interest. In a "singles bar," interest in the opposite sex is indicated by trying to catch the other person's eye. Continued eye contact can be highly suggestive.

Eye behavior is far more important in communication than most people realize. People gaze towards those whom they like, and avert their eyes to avoid feedback. Eyes drop when touchy subjects arise or when embarrassed. People usually look away from those they dislike or with whom they feel uncomfortable for any number of reasons. We may look down or away when avoiding the truth or speaking to someone we feel is superior. The culture instills much of our head and eye behavior.

Generally, the confident employee looks at the person being spoken to. Looking at a guest while speaking to them is something every good employee learns, a habit that can be cultivated and that can improve communication.

In customer relations, direct eye contact with a smile is

usually best.

The Smile

Once eye contact or eye-to-face contact has been made, smile. It precedes or goes with a greeting. It sets the stage for customer relations, preparing the players, inviting cordiality and reducing apprehensions. It creates value at no cost, enriching those who receive it and taking nothing from those who give it. It is given in a flash but the effects can be lasting.

A smile can disarm the hostile and reassure the timid.

Like all aphorisms, these are not without qualification. There are silly smiles, smirks, nervous smiles, superior smiles, disdainful smiles, and so on. The friendly smile, though, is almost always welcome.

The Handshake

According to anthropologists, the handshake may have originated early in evolution as a gesture, hands outstretched, palms exposed, to show that no weapon was being carried. In some societies, the handshake is expected in even a casual meeting — to neglect it is a serious social affront. In other societies a person of lower social status always waits for the higher-status person to initiate the handshake.

When appropriate, handshaking serves to reassure and may be seen as a display of good will. Handshaking is part of the touching/brushing phenomenon. When a person seen as one of equal or higher status offers to shake hands, the other person is likely to be pleased. Not so if the overture is made by a person seen as being decidedly of lower status.

Should the gentleman hold out his hand to a lady or should he wait for the lady to make the first move? This depends upon good judgment. In the past, the gentleman did not make the handshake overture. If, however, the lady seems shy or ill at ease, the gentleman could appropriately make the first move.

When the occasion calls for handshaking, do it appropriately. Not the limp grip, not the iron grip. But:

— Look at the person while shaking hands.

— Present a firm grip.

— Present the same handshake regardless of gender — don't give a woman the dead-fish handshake just because of her gender.

In a business introduction the other person wants you to be reassuring and confident. He or she does not want to be intimidated or overpowered.

Social and Psychological Distance

How much "social distance" does the guest need? How close physically should a service person be to the guest? Does the guest expect formality and reserve? Needs for social distance vary greatly from one person to another.

Anthropologists have learned that the desirable physical distance between people conversing together varies with the cultural background of the individual. Latin Americans and Middle Easterners often feel uneasy unless physically close to whomever they speak. Others, British and Eastern North Americans for example, feel uncomfortable if approached too closely. Men are inclined to stand closer to other men when talking; also men and women communicating stand close. But, women communicating with other women stand farther apart. Older persons move away from close quarters usually because, with age, they become more farsighted and have difficulty seeing clearly if closer than about 20 inches of another person.

What about social distance? Persons who are concerned with status and position want "social distance" between themselves and anyone they consider less elevated. Examples:

A flight attendant on an American airline flight approached a well-dressed woman and her companion flying first class from the Argentine to New York City and asked, "May I serve you a beverage?"

The woman stared ahead, no reply.

The flight attendant, thinking the woman had not heard, repeated the question, whereupon the man sitting in the next seat leaned forward and said, "My wife never speaks to the servants."

Obviously the Argentinian woman was quite prepared to be rude in order to maintain what she perceived as a correct social distance.

A guest at a mountain resort informed the manager that he would never return to the hotel.

"Why not?"

"My bed was not turned down last evening by the maid."

The guest was telling the manager that he, the guest, was of a social class that required turn-down service, a service ordinarily provided by luxury hotels.

Informality may be called for, or just the opposite.

Regional Custom Education and Expectation

Custom and expectation to a large extent determine the degree of formality the guest expects.

Accents, vocabulary and phraseology are associated with educational level, geographical area and social class. The phrase "Thank you so much" is associated with a higher educational and class level than "Thank you very much." Some people feel that "Thank you so much," which is more formal, is affected.

People from the Midwest are likely to say "Thank you very much"; large-city dwellers tend to be more abrupt, but no less sincere. It may be appropriate in the deep South to use "Ma'am" instead of Madam when addressing women; male guests are referred to as gentlemen, never as "this man," "this chap," "this guy," or "this fellow."

Some guests are easier to please and be pleasant to than others. An obvious statement, to be sure, but there are subtleties. An old, bleary-eyed person may elicit compassion, or contempt. It is easy to be pleasant to the attractive person. How about the person who is considered unattractive by today's standards?

The class of clientele, in part, determines where lies that thin line between being friendly and overfamiliar with the guest. Knowing the correct social distance is a precious skill in interpersonal relations, a mark of sensitivity and intelligence. What constitutes familiarity varies widely with the individual. The perceptive employee recognizes clues signaling when to approach, when to back off.

When an employee is encroaching on another's "social space," the guest may look embarrassed, stare ahead, or answer abruptly. The employee may be overstepping the social barrier. Perhaps silly, but important to most.

Alexander Hamilton once took a dare to put his arm around President George Washington, and did so. A response followed — so glacial that Hamilton said had he known the response he never would have attempted such familiarity.

Openness and informal friendliness vary with geography, increasing proportionally as the distance increases from large Eastern and Northern cities, to the South and to the West. Hotel clerks and salespersons in Boston behave, in general, much more formally than those in Las Vegas or Los Angeles.

Depending on the price, some guests, especially the "newly rich," expect and demand deference from all "staff"; others are embarrassed by it.

An employee who asks "What does this person need?" gains insight into the role expected and the part to play that will be most acceptable to the guest.

Posture

The guest has no way of knowing the real service person. The guest notices dress, posture, alertness or lack of it, attentiveness or lack of it, confidence or lack of it. The guest notices vivacity, friendliness and general health. There is no way, however, for the guest to know the true feelings of the service employee.

The way a person stands or sits, slumped or leaning on something, slouched or upright, including alertness or indifference, indicates much about that person. Within limits, good posture can be learned. A hypertense person usually shows tension by being overly erect, stiff and sometimes hunched up, with the neck forward. Confidence and ease of manner are reflected in the way a person sits, stands and walks.

Behavioral scientists have stated that acting in a certain manner has repercussions mentally. Act confident and confidence builds. Act depressed and depression sets in. Act friendly and the tendency for friendliness develops. Stand erect and ready and the mind reacts more quickly. Psychologists have set up training programs in which a person learns to hold his or her head high, sit and stand easily, and avoid the type of posture which is uncomfortable for mind and body.

Tension

Standing in an overly tense manner is tiring and slows the supply of blood to the brain. Watch a military formation standing at attention for any length of time and, sure enough, one or more soldiers faint and fall to the ground. Persons working on their feet should learn techniques to avoid overtiring certain muscles. Moving about helps, bending periodically and lifting the head to relieve strained muscles.

Watch for clues of tension, e.g., sweaty palms, perspiration on the forehead, quivering lips, heightening of voice, leaning too far forward, pain in the back of the neck or shoulders, pain in the small of the back. When tensions rise, do what is necessary to reduce them, e.g., lower the voice, slow the speech.

How much tension is too much?

Most of us enjoy being excited - up to a point. Hyperactivity becomes unpleasant. What is an optimal level of excitement for the average person? How long can excitement be sustained without an energy letdown? How much adrenalin is right for a particular situation? Individuals vary tremendously in the degree of excitement and tension which can be sustained over a period of time, and it should be remembered that each situation calls for an appropriate excitement level - neither too high nor too low. A professional football player has to be on a "high" to mobilize the utmost energy. The same level of excitement in a salesperson would leave that person dragging after an hour or so. Too much excitement interferes with critical thinking; too little excitement and the person becomes listless and apathetic.

Biorhythms and the Service Employee

Each service person has his or her own appropriate daily rhythm. It is a good idea for employees keep in step with his or her own personal biorhythm. Some people are morning persons; others are late-night persons. It takes time to change the established rhythm. Most people become affected by adrenalin production early in the morning, which has the effect of awakening them and causing them to get up and out of bed. Some people become alert only after several cups of coffee. Energy and productivity is usually high until midmorning, then a break is called for to recharge. Productivity and excitement sustain themselves until the lunch period.

Body temperature and glandular activity follow rhythms. Body temperature, for example, is lowest about 3 o'clock in the morning for most people. Once the pattern has been established with the ups and downs, rhythm of excitement and less excitement, biological clocks inside the body keep it going in the same manner. Knowing one's personal rhythm helps in anticipating ups and downs.

The afternoon starts off a little lower than the morning high and trails off until time to quit. Often there is a spurt of excitement just before the end of the shift.

It is not possible to exist without a certain amount of problem solving, tension and, from time to time, excessive excitement or stress. What is stressful to one may be someone else's challenge. When problems seem unsolvable or inescapable, stress is almost inevitable. Problems that can be solved without excessive anxiety are challenges. Excessive tension equates with stress.

Excitement

Excitement is pleasant, up to a point. Excessive excitement impairs judgment and efficient motor reactions. Excitement is related to the flow of adrenalin and to the "fight or flight" reaction considered to be instinctive in all animal life. As humans evolved, adrenalin was needed to stimulate the body for emergency reactions. In a civilized society, however, people usually neither "fight" nor "flee" from a frightening situation. The body is prepared to run, but it does not because of acquired self-discipline, specific training and society's expectations. If the brain is overloaded with electrical charges, a person may panic and say and do things that might be regretted.

At a meeting of hotel and restaurant educators, one highly-respected professor became so furious that he hit and knocked down one of his conferees. That incident was never forgotten by those who saw or heard of it.

One way to look at excessive tension (stress) is to think of the brain as functioning in an organized and systematic way under normal conditions. Under excessive stress, the organization and circuitry is overloaded. Logic and rational thought is overwhelmed.

Common sense causes us either to avoid stresses that cannot be handled or to learn ways of changing the situation (if possible) to reduce the effects.

Service personnel need a certain level of alertness to come across as interested and responsive. The reservationist who is half asleep on the phone comes across as being slow and uncaring. The fatigued receptionist, cashier or server sends signals that, at best, are interpreted as "half-hearted." On the other hand, the over-excited service person makes mistakes and appears jumpy or erratic.

Service people who are on their feet hour after hour may have a problem of over-fatiguing certain muscles, especially those of the back. When an activity exceeds the tolerance level of the individual, pathologic anatomical changes take place in the skeletal muscle system. This is stress. The blood supply to some muscles is decreased (ischemia). If this occurs over a period of time, excessive fibrous tissue (fibrosis) is formed in the muscle and chronic pain results.

Athletes find that often they try too hard and need to relax more. Putting too much effort into a skill or movement is often counterproductive. When a receptionist, server or other service employee tries too hard, it is readily noticeable and often makes the guest uncomfortable. Excessive, chronic stress leads to illness.

Stress reduction can be achieved with a variety of activities that may vary from person to person: reading the paper, walking, watching an interesting television program, riding a bicycle, stamp collecting, using a computer.

Stress reduction by trying regular, moderate exercise is well-known. Equally well-known is the fact that the human body must move or it will deteriorate. "Use it or lose it." People must use energy to generate further energy. Paradoxically, exercise is said to be nature's best tranquilizer. Several studies support the view that regular exercise sensitizes and enlarges the adrenal glands to provide more reserves and makes responses more efficient.

Excess tension begets more tension. Symptoms include

frowning, teeth clenching and the forcing the tongue to the roof of the mouth. Clenched hands, quick, shallow breathing or frequent gasping also indicate excessive stress.

One way to reduce unwanted stress is to identify the things, situations or people that are stress-producing. Stephan R. Germeroth divides stressors into those that are manageable and those that are beyond individual control. Some stressors are inevitable, but they can be viewed in a less injurious way. The ones that are manageable he calls "The Negotiables." An example: avoid those things, people or situations that produce excess stress and can be avoided. Others are non-negotiables.[3]

Examples of Negotiables	Examples of Non-Negotiables
Stress-producing persons, places and situations which can be avoided.	Things over which one has no control, such as nuclear war, the aging process, a particular in-law, the weather, a boss who owns the company.
Better time management.	
Minimal major changes in life.	
Regular, moderate exercise.	
Proper eating habits.	

Fear of public speaking, fear of dealing with powerful people, fear of flying and a variety of other fears can be overcome. Many fears can be avoided. If fear of being mugged or raped makes life miserable, better to move or change jobs. If fear of becoming ill in a less developed country raises tension, better take the vacation in a place where health hazards are fewer.

Some fear is nearly always there: fear of failure: concern over not doing the proper thing; and fear of not measuring up to expectation are widespread fears. A certain amount of fear is stimulating. Excessive fear is debilitating. Long-lasting anxiety produces tension that often shows as physical

University
of Ulster
LIBRARY

impairment.

Harnessed tension, tension directed toward a well-defined goal, can be pleasurable. The tension level should approximate the need for it. One level is appropriate in case of fire, another for calmly taking a reservation or registering a guest or seating a restaurant customer. Much depends upon the leader, dining room manager, front desk manager, whichever party is seen to be in charge. Let that person panic and the attention level explodes, inappropriate for sound judgment or correct action. If the leader is anxious, the group becomes restive and anxious as well. A calm leader tends to calm the work group. A confident leader lends confidence to others. Because managers' stress levels are so easily picked up by others, the manager who is overwrought should withdraw until composure is regained. Auguste Escoffier, "the chef of kings and the king of chefs," took a walk around the block when he felt he was getting overexcited.

Some employees relish keeping the emotional pot boiling in the workplace and work at "disturbing the peace." High-strung individuals tend to cause tension in those around them. They are "tension carriers," perhaps without intending to be so.

One manager tells what he does when the symptoms of excessive stress appear:

"I keep my mouth closed and drag my jaw down. I place my tongue low in my mouth. If out of public view, I stop, close my eyes and lower my top eyelids — and for a brief moment breathe slowly and enjoy the darkness."

Stimulants, such as caffeine in coffee and soft drinks, can alter the rhythms and pep the person up for a brief time. A cup of coffee or a cola drink may be needed to perk the system up for a special need to get through a period of time. Physicians warn, however, that caffeine or any other stimulant or depressant can be addictive and self-defeating in the long run.

The smart service person tries to anticipate the natural

rhythms and work with them.

Pacing

Recognizing one's individual rhythm and living with it is a form of pacing. Knowing when to accelerate and when to slack off is valuable in customer relations, so that one does not become hyperactive or overtired. An excellent policy to follow is to rest before becoming tired. In other words, do not wait until fatigue has set in to think about slacking off. Once fatigue has set in, recovery takes longer. This is especially true with older persons.

The Challenge

Guest relations can be fun and also demanding, calling for flexibility, patience and an abundance of self-control.

Too often the person who says "I would like to work in a hotel restaurant because I like people" really means "I like nice people." The work often calls for dealing with people who are under stress, angry, tired or boring as well as the "nice people."

If either party, the employee or guest, is fatigued or is under pressure, the challenge of making guest relations pleasant increases.

Guest relations involve the never-ending search for more effective interpersonal relations, concern for the other person's well-being, awareness of that person's frame of mind, state of fatigue and psychological needs at the moment. Knowing what to say, how and when to say it, and when to be quiet, has always been a highly prized skill, one that smoothes human relations, avoids unnecessary tension and friction between people and adds to the pleasure of living.

ENDNOTES

1. Judith Martin, "Common Courtesy", Atheneum, (New York), 1985.

2. American Hotel & Motel Association, *Lodging Magazine,* AH & MA, (New York), 1977.

3. McGuigan, F. J., et al., An edited article, "Improved Stress Management and Tension Control: A Model Program in a Community College," *Stress and Tension Control*, (New York), Plenum Press, 1984.

CHAPTER 3

GUEST RELATIONS WITH "THE FRONT OF THE HOUSE"

Front of the House Operations refers to those operations where face-to-face contact with the guest is normally expected. "Back of the House" areas, such as engineering, kitchen, housekeeping, etc., may have occasional guest contact but such contact is not normally expected.

The front desk of a hotel or motel is usually the primary nexus between guest and hotel or motel. The person working the front desk, whatever the job title — front desk clerk, receptionist, guest service agent — is a person who registers and checks the guest in and out, keeps records by hand or computer, relates to the housekeeping and other departments, and generally operates an information and record center. Although concerns may arise which are directly related to some other department, it is usually the front desk where the guest contact is made, regardless of the nature of the problem or concern.

The Desk Clerk/Receptionist

Desk clerks in hotels or motels are often the first people to greet incoming guests. They register the guests, assign a room to them, issue the room key, and often provide information about services available in the hotel and in the community. When guests check out, desk clerks receive payment of their accounts and inform the housekeeper that a vacant room is ready for cleaning. Records must be kept of reservations, rooms occupied and guests' accounts. Desk clerks also receive and distribute mail, telegrams and parcels and, in large hotels, may supervise the bellhop, doorman, telephone operator or cashier. The day is divided into three shifts, each eight hours in length, which means that desk clerks work very little overtime but their working hours are irregular, and days off won't necessarily be on the weekend. On the night shift, desk clerks in smaller hotels may act as assistant manager, night cashier or night auditor. They must stand for the majority of their working hours. Since desk clerks provide one of the first impressions of the hotel's hospitality, they must have a pleasant manner, tact and more than average patience. Part-time and summer vacation experience as a desk clerk is valuable when seeking permanent employment. Most hotels prefer to hire people who have at least a high school diploma.

In APPENDIX A, the Job Description for a front desk clerk/receptionist is shown in detail. Job descriptions and definitions of other positions involved with primary guest contact and guest relations are also given.

Guest Histories and Guest Relations

Guest Histories are constructed and filed for future use in preparing for guest return visits. This allows the hotel staff to recognize the guest in a more personal way. The effect is similar to that of remembering a person's name after a long absence. Maintaining guest histories is time-consuming, however, and is usually done by luxury properties where guests are likely to return year after year.

Guest information, including individual likes and dislikes, previous visits, current addresses and bits of personal information are assembled into what are called guest histories, such as: wife plays tennis; will need a foursome for golf; will order "Brut" Champagne for dinner; usually departs before 6:00 a.m.

Prior to the computer, manual files were kept on guests,

especially in luxury hotels and the old-style resort hotels. Reservations clerks, and many times the owners, would make personal notes about their guests for reference in writing personal and promotional letters (such as for future golf or tennis tournaments). Guest histories could be voluminous and the time needed to keep them current extensive. With the advent of computers, information about thousands of guests can be entered and the information retrieved whenever needed. The work may be assigned to one or several reservation clerks or may be a part of the duties of guest relations personnel. Punching a few keys can produce a full record of an individual guest, home address, business affiliation phone numbers, date of last visit to hotel, food and beverage preferences and other information which can be used in making the guest feel welcome and important.

A glance at a guest history tells the desk clerk previous room rates, preferred location in the hotel and a variety of other information useful at registration.

There is no doubt that guests appreciate being treated as individuals and are flattered by the personal attention based on guest history files.

Name Magic

A number of luxury hotels have arranged for guest names to be used in every guest contact. Quite a feat in a 300-room hotel, but done nevertheless. It might be called "name magic." Happiness may be hearing one's name used with respect and seeing it spelled correctly. When a guest registers, the safe thing to do is to print the name over the signature, spelling out the name and asking if the spelling is correct.

One's name is something personal, even when it is Smith. Some people are name sensitive and become very much upset if "Smythe" is mistakenly spelled or pronounced "Smith." The name takes on a magical quality, invested by the owner with some of the person's own attributes, a partial extension of the personality. Ms. Smythe does not want to be confused with Ms. Smith. And, of course, Mr. Ruiz expects everyone to pronounce his name in good Spanish, "Roo-ese" (accent on the second syllable).

Name magic is somehow destroyed if the name is mispronounced, confused or misspelled. The person making the error is seen as unsophisticated, uninterested or rude. Take the time to use, and use often, the magic associated with names. And don't be funny, even if the name is Attila Fundrick, Mr. Jerk or Ralph Simple.

There is also *reverse* name magic. The employee with first name suitably engraved in a name tag is much more likely to be addressed by name than by "psssst" or "hey, you."

Titles Ring Nicely

Though many establishments feature informality, most of us are quite ready to be called by whatever title is appropriate. Applying titles can be a little sticky at times, but it is better to err on the side of formality until asked to be less formal.

Europeans are especially concerned with and attentive to titles. The German wife may be called Mrs. Director Konig if her husband is or has been a director of a school or bank. European titles are too complicated to worry about on the American scene except for the obvious ones. Sir and Madam cover most situations, unless the title or preferred address is known. If known, use it.

Medical doctors and doctors of philosophy and education also enjoy the use of their titles. Once the title is used, it is perfectly reasonable to revert to, Mister and Madam, Sir and Ma'am.

The British, much taken with rank, title all members of peerage with the rank of baron through that of marquis. Lords, for example, are "Lord Derby" or "Lord Somebody." Dukes are known as Dukes and in formal correspondence as "Your Grace." Knights and baronets get the formal "Sir John Wilson."

Military officers, too, are pleased to hear their titles, especially if commanders, colonels and above. Lt. Commanders and Commanders in the Navy are both called Commander. Lt. Colonels and Colonels in the Army, Air Force and Marine Corp. are called Colonel.

A rule of thumb: If the title is used in correspondence, its use will probably be welcome in person. Academic deans like to be called Dean; professors like to be called Professor; dentists like to be called Doctor. But don't overdo it: "Yes Doctor," "No, Doctor," "Beautiful day, Professor," begins to sound like something out of a Gilbert and Sullivan operetta.

Foreign visitors are likely to expect more formality than North Americans. "Good morning, Mr. Smith" is better received than plain "Good morning" and many foreign visitors expect employees not to make the first overture in speaking unless it is something highly neutral such as "Good Afternoon, Mr. Smith."

Spanish names can be confusing since the individual uses his or her name plus that of the family's. A husband and wife might register as follows: Jorge Gonzalez y Sanchez. Gonzalez is his mother's family name; Sanchez is his father's family name. If traveling alone, his wife might register, Rosa Calvado de Sanchez. Calvado is her father's family name.

Phrase Magic

In guest relations, three phrases take on almost magical qualities:

"May I help you?"

"Thank you."

"I'm very sorry."

When used, each of these phrases implies concern for the other person, recognition of that person and respect for that person — in a word, courtesy.

Even though a guest may obviously be in the wrong — and

know it — saying "I'm sorry" may be interpreted as "Yes, I understand and sympathize."

Of course, the tone of the voice can destroy the magic. "Thank you" can come across as an insult. Any expression can be cast as sarcasm. The look, the tone of voice and the attentiveness determine the emotional load.

The word "please" also has the magic quality when used sincerely and with concern. Requests made to a guest — or to a fellow employee — are enhanced by prefacing or ending the request with a "Please."

There's also magic in these words:

"Welcome back."

"We're happy you're here."

"I trust you are well."

"Sorry to have kept you waiting."

"I am as close as the telephone."

"I'm sorry, I'll correct it at once."

"Have a nice trip home."

The tone of voice and voice inflection may be more important than the words used. A lilting "Good morning" does a great deal more than a "Good morning" spoken in monotone. "Hello" with a rising inflection on the last syllable suggests optimism and expectancy. "Hello" with the last syllable dropped can come across as "I'd rather not say anything" or even "I'd rather not be here." "Hello" over the phone can come through with an eagerness or sound like "You're bothering me."

Are You Coming Through?

Speaking and listening make up a large part of guest relations. Can both be improved? Of course, just as almost every human activity can be analyzed and improved. Actors are forever studying their speaking patterns.

Much of the way one is perceived by others is determined by the manner of speech, the rate of speech, the tone of voice, the choice of words and the responsiveness displayed in conversation. These and other aspects of speaking can be improved.

The tone of voice suggests the range of emotion: frustration, excitement, joy, anger, resignation or disinterest.

Rate of speech and voice pitch can be changed. The high-strung individual who speaks too rapidly can learn to slow down, just as the stammerer can learn to speak slowly and clearly. A woman with a deep voice can pitch her tone up, while the shrill notes of a speaker who tends to screech can be lowered. Modulated speech is something that every actor learns.

When tension builds, speaking tends to become abbreviated, as though shot out of a cannon, much too fast for tired, distracted or elderly guests. Quite naturally, a busy establishment means the employee is pumped up, and necessarily so, to meet the demands of the job. Adrenalin flows, the eyes brighten, the pupils dilate, and the speech becomes staccato. The employee must make a conscious effort to back off and to measure how he or she is coming through to the customer. With older guests it may be necessary to repeat what is said, but do it graciously by saying the same thing in a slightly different way. An example:

"You pay your bill at the cashier's counter, Sir." (With a pause, the guest looks puzzled).

"The cashier's counter is right over there, Sir."

Avoid Curtness

An employee may sound curt without meaning to.

In the press of business it is quite natural to abbreviate responses and questions to the point of curtness. Often it is better to slow down and to say more, repeating the same information in different words.

"What time must I check out of the hotel?

The answer might be, "Twelve o'clock."

Better to say, "Our policy is to ask all guests to vacate their rooms by noon. Otherwise there is an additional charge."

"The bus leaves in 10 minutes" may convey the essential information needed. Is this more gracious?: "Your limousine will probably be at the front of the hotel in about 10 minutes. You might check with the bell captain for further information."

In a busy establishment, you may be distracted or too eager to get on with the job to listen closely to what the guest says. The proverbial little old lady may ask,

"Where is the ladies' retiring room?"

"Just sit anywhere in the lobby."

The lady may be asking directions to the ladies' room. It takes skill in a busy establishment to ensure that the person you are addressing feels your entire attention at the instant of communication. Good eye contact can help in this matter.

Repeat for Clarity When Important

When something important is said, there is little recourse other than to ask for a reiteration or to repeat back what is said:

Guest to hotel: "Please wake me at seven o'clock tomorrow morning." The hotel receptionist: "Yes, Ma'am, I am leaving a wake-up call for seven o'clock tomorrow morning."

Elderly people, foreigners, and preoccupied people may need to have information repeated several times. To avoid appearing didactic, vary the information somewhat.

When necessary, go slowly, be patient and repeat the same information in a slightly different manner. Saying more may not be efficient but adds a note of graciousness to the conversation:

"What time do you close?"

The answer might be, "Five."

Better to say, "On weekdays we close at six o'clock. Saturdays and Sundays at five."

Being excessively precise and emphatic can be construed as belligerence. A well-modulated voice, well-paced sentences and the use of a few extra words is often better received than direct, efficient sentences.

Active Listening

One mark of attention and concern for the other person is to listen attentively and to react in some way. The mere fact of listening is recognition of a sort, recognition that the person is important, that what is said is being reacted to and registered. Even though what is said may not be logical — or even rational — that person is telling the listener something: a feeling, a concern, a helplessness, hostility, warmth, indifference, disdain or a need for understanding.

The employee need not agree or disagree with what is said, only react. When hostility or a grievance is expressed, the safest reaction is to restate what was said or to comment on the feeling expressed. Example:

"I have been waiting here for 15 minutes."

"I'm sorry you had to wait, and I can understand your annoyance."

In PART II, more will be said about the technique of Active Listening and several exercises will be presented to assist the reader in developing the technique.

Problems in Listening

The great temptation in listening is to cut in. Normal speech proceeds at about 100 words a minute. Thought is much faster, about 400 words a minute. It is easy to mentally race ahead of a speaker and cut in with your own brilliant thoughts. Doing so is discourteous.

Actively hearing tends to decline with age and many people are hard of hearing even when young. Cues relating to this disability may be picked up from the way a person listens. If the head is cocked toward the sound or the speaker, and if the eyes are focused on the speaker's lips, the person may be trying to compensate for hearing loss. In such cases, the speaker should be careful to face the person so that lip reading and maximum hearing is possible. In other words, don't turn away from someone you suspect of having a hearing deficiency. Speak directly to the person and perhaps louder than usual. In giving directions, it may help to ask indirect questions to learn if the person has actually received the information.

"To get to the theater you will be turning on which street?"

"Do you have enough information to get there?"

"Would you like for me to repeat that or write it down?"

When You Don't Hear

If something is not heard and seems important, say something like:

"Pardon Me?" or, "I'm sorry, I did not hear what you said." Adding a smile softens the request. When not sure of the name just spoken. "Would you spell that for me, please?"

Only a boor says, "Huh?"

What?" can come across as too abrupt or demanding.

"Would you mind repeating that?" is probably better than, "Say that again, please."

Should the guest speak too softly, the clerk may have to suggest: "Would you please speak a little louder?" Never "I can't hear you."

Facing the person and focusing on the speaker's lips can help. Sometimes it may be better to miss some part of what is being said than to ask the person to repeat it.

More will be said about Active Listening in Part II. There is also an exercise in the APPENDIX that will be explained later as more detail regarding Active Listening is presented.

Watch Those Pauses

Pauses in conversation — by phone or face-to-face — may be construed differently than intended. The speaker may be thinking and pausing to reflect. The listener may take the pause as disagreement with what has just been said. A pause can be intended to question what has been said, an unexpressed question to which the listener may or may not respond.

Relating to Different Age Groups

A common saying: "Everyone is different" may be true, but also people tend to fall into classifications, holding similar values and having similar needs. Knowing or at least tentatively placing a person in a particular age bracket helps in relating to the person. A valuable clue to a person's value system is his or her age.

During the formative years, events have influenced values differently decade by decade. Those who went to high school during the 1930s and experienced the Depression have different values than younger generations. Those who experienced World War II in their formative years were affected by the war and the coming of the communications revolution. The radicalism of the 1960s produced still another set of values.

It is difficult to pinpoint a person's age, but placing the person in a general age bracket also places the person on the value spectrum. The child of the Depression is likely to place a higher value on money and perhaps has little respect for the big spender. Those who grew up in affluence after the 1950s are usually more ready to buy a luxury item without experiencing the guilt feeling the older generation may feel.

"What you are, where you were when." The sentence is

not a conundrum, but is supposed to make one think of the imprint of values of a particular time period on the personality.

The clever person picks up little clues and responds to them appropriately. The older person may expect more deference than the younger person. "Sir" or "Madam" may be just right for one customer but completely wrong for another. The service person can test an approach, then quickly shift it if it is not well received.

Marathon Talkers

The nonstop talker just loves to converse, to tell you about the family, the weather, the grandchild, the stomach ailment and so on. Tact and patience may be the only answer to get away from such persons without hurting their feelings. Marathon talkers seldom realize the imposition they are placing on others, but it is rude to cut them off abruptly. Sometimes it is necessary to explain that you are sorry, but you must do this or that to care for other customers. Apologize and excuse yourself. Remember to be polite.

Relating to the Boor

Once in a while, patience is put to a severe test when a showoff appears who tries to attract attention and boost his or her own importance by speaking loudly, laughing crudely, telling off-color stories or generally acting the boor. The dictionary defines a boor as rude or insensitive. The person may have good reason for needing to attract attention in such a manner. Psychologists maintain that most such behavior springs from a sense of inferiority and the need to compensate for it. Too bad more civilized ways are not employed. The well-bred service person shows his or her breeding by maintaining civility and ignoring as much as possible crude remarks and loutish behavior. Perhaps the person has been drinking or is on drugs. Dealing with people who are irrational is indeed frustrating and demanding. Ignoring the person may be a solution. Sometimes firmness is the only solution, in which case, eye contact is most important. If worse comes to worst, management may have to be called in to help.

The Front Desk Clerk/Receptionist as a Focus of Hostility

As every clerk/receptionist knows, being at the front desk is not all fun and games. All the more reason to develop the habit of "grace under pressure." Anything that goes wrong in the hotel may be and often is associated with the clerk/receptionist even though that person may have absolutely no control over what has happened. The clerk/receptionist is visible, associated with management, accessible and the obvious person to whom to direct complaints:

The TV isn't working.

The hot water is too hot.

The hot water is too cold.

There is no hot water.

There is only one clean towel.

The toilet paper has run out.

The bed is too hard.

The bed is too soft.

There is no ice in the machine.

The soda machine does not work.

The room is too cold.

The room is too hot.

There is no stationery in the room.

Why don't you handle stamps at the front desk?

Why can't I cash a large check?

The list is endless.

The guest may be right or wrong.

The clerk/receptionist may be the only management representative on the premises and becomes the surrogate manager.

Projecting Confidence and Reassurance

In guest relations it is important to display confidence in self and professional skill. The guest, often tired, sometimes bewildered, steps into the establishment needing to find a person whose behavior says "I am glad you are here. I know what you want and will do everything I can to help you."

The employee after several hours on the job may feel anything but confident and buoyant. He or she may be just as tired as the guest, more frustrated, shoulders sagging, back aching, and feet in pain but, nevertheless, should try to act self-assured. Straighten the shoulders. Smile. Keep the voice level and, if necessary, speak deliberately and kindly.

The role is not easy, especially in a busy hotel or restaurant where there is perhaps a line of guests. The employee cannot take the time, but brusqueness offends the guest.

A confidence role is easier when practiced and can even be fun when guests and their problems are considered a challenge.

Making a Charge Adjustment

When making any kind of a charge adjustment or listening to a complaint, which could lead to an adjustment or refund, attentive listening is the preferred response. Often the guest does not really expect to receive what is being requested, or even demanded. But the person does expect a hearing, and expects it regardless of how farfetched the request may be.

Sometimes the guest has simply forgotten some aspect of the matter which leads to it. A request for adjustment on the hotel bill and a ready explanation is quickly accepted. It is possible to be too generous in making refunds or adjustments, and it must be recognized that there are people who play games with a business trying to get more than is reasonable or equitable. In a large hotel, for example, the front desk staff was making adjustments to the tune of $25,000 a month, agreeing with every guest who stated an adjustment was due. Later, when a more firm policy was enforced, adjustments were reduced by half. Guests were still satisfied that they had been treated fairly. Good guest relations does not necessarily mean a lack of firmness. With regard to house policy rules when dealing with guest complaints, some suggestions are in order:

1. Repeat the complaint. Too often, the exact nature of the complaint is misunderstood. Unnecessary confusion and complications can result.

2. Apologize. It costs nothing to apologize, even though the employee may have had nothing to do with the cause of the complaint. This credits the complainer with being honest and bright enough to have a legitimate complaint (though this may not be true); the guest will ordinarily appreciate the response.

3. Empathize. The complaint itself may be of no substance, or worse, not even legitimate, but the complainer expects and usually appreciates a reasonable hearing.

4. Take positive action. Business policy may limit what any particular employee can do. Positive action may be only to refer the complainant to a supervisor. Don't leave the customer hanging.

5. Express appreciation. This may be more ritualistic than real. Yet we should appreciate learning where service or product can be improved.

The Chronic Complainer

There are such people and they are a real challenge. Perhaps all they want is extra attention. If so, try to give it to them up to a point. When that point arrives, you may have to turn the person over to a supervisor. Try not to get upset yourself.

The Angry Guest

Don't let angry guests trap you into getting angry too. It's your decision to get angry - or to stay detached. This is a form of "game playing" and will be addressed in detail in PART II under "The Games People Play." When someone is trying to play a game by causing an uproar:

Listen attentively.

Do not act or imply that the customer is wrong (even when he/she is).

Say you are sorry (you may only be sorry that he or she is upset).

Try to be of assistance.

If you cannot help, get someone who can. Introduce the guest and leave graciously.

The Guest is Never Wrong (Well, Hardly Ever)

Actually the guest is wrong as much as anyone else. The question is, however, would you rather be right, or would you rather have a satisfied guest? Tact in dealing with guests means that, for appearances' sake, the guest never makes a mistake. Even if a guest has misunderstood certain directions and is entirely wrong, it is often better to take the blame and say, "I am sorry. I was not clear."

In other words, by assuming the burden of error, the guest is relieved of embarrassment. One important rule worth repeating: never try to win an argument or make a point. You and the business always lose in the long run. Also, if the discussion gets heated, or to a point that it can no longer be handled in a satisfactory manner, refer the guest to a supervisor.

Obviously, the guest may be wrong, but the guest is still the guest and should not be embarrassed. "Wrongness" is a state of mind. It may have little or no relation to facts. The guest is right if he or she believes so. Down deep, the guest may know he or she is wrong or, at least, partly wrong. Let the guest save face. If possible, assume "the mistake" and let the guest off the hook.

Positive recognition of guests is a form of respect. Ignoring or trivializing them is an insult.

Your Friend, the Complainer?

The guest who tells you about bad service or poor quality may be an establishment's best customer.

Remember that the person who is assertive or even aggressive has made an emotional investment in the operation of the establishment. The 95 percent who walk away and say nothing after receiving bad service are doing you a disservice. In addition, most such guests don't come back again. Making a fuss in public takes courage, and may be an act of kindness if seen in the light of calling attention to things that can be corrected.

When guests complain, they usually are not wasting your time!

Providing Guest Information

Providing information is a service that builds public goodwill. Providing incomplete information can be worse than none at all. How many times have guests asked directions and been given information that only serves to confuse?

"To get to Highway 10, turn left at the corner and go three lights. Then right on to the highway."

Turn left from which corner? Where is the guest parked?

Another common mistake in giving directions:

"Just go north five blocks and turn right."

Just go north? Which way is north?

Few things are quite so exasperating to a guest who would like to drive out of town as when, upon asking an employee how to do it, the reply is: "I don't drive," or "I don't know."

It doesn't matter if the employee does not drive; all service employees should know the routes and general information about the locale.

A tip about giving directions: have a supply of local and state maps available and a large felt pen with which to trace out routes on the maps for guests seeking directions. Maps are often supplied by the Chamber of Commerce, car rental agencies, oil companies, tourist bureaus and convention and visitors' centers. If, indeed, maps cannot be had except by purchase, say so, and ask the inquirer if he or she would like to buy one. Know the best routes for getting to major points of interest, airports and the like. Avoid giving the guest a choice of routes; it is difficult enough to learn one when a stranger in a community. Also, give the guest the simplest route — not the more complicated one, even if it's faster.

What kind of information should be made available? Some of the information suggested below may be applicable. Each hotel countertop has its own "bible" of information, anticipating commonly asked questions.

General Information

Information on public transport routes, fares, schedules and instructions on how to operate ticket machines.

City maps and lists of attractions.

Museums and zoos — hours, admission charges.

Major attractions — hours and charges.

History of area and information about its leading businesses, recreational activities and civic organizations.

Meeting places and times of service clubs such as Rotary and Kiwanis.

Restaurants, types of cuisine, etc.

Houses of worship of all religions and times of service.

Information about local arts and crafts, typical products for souvenirs.

Tape recorders and cassettes for local walking tours.

Walking tour brochure and map.

List of nearby stores and shops with multilingual staffs.

Information about factory outlets and bargain stores.

Maps and descriptions of one-day and several-day countryside driving tours.

Local plant tours.

Sightseeing and limousine service with multilingual drivers.

Postage scale - knowledge of overseas and airmail rates.

Stamps - over the counter and not by machine, so that guests can get only the denominations they want and pay no more than the face value of the stamps.

Addresses and phone numbers of foreign embassies or consulates.

Clear, concise guides to city or area, cultural activities, calendars of events, sports schedules, etc.

Conversation tables, clothing size equivalents, etc.

Car rental - location of agencies, rates and procedures.

Information on distances between various points in the United States, time to travel between them by various modes, time to allow between hotel and airport, etc.

Foreign currency exchange chart.

Local cultural exchange agencies.

Time differences between American cities and major world capitals to aid the visitor in planning overseas phone calls.

Names, addresses and phone numbers of hospitals and local medical and dental associations, with particular attention to those with foreign language capabilities.

List of multilingual stenographers.

Foreign newspapers and magazines available locally.

Local foreign language radio stations and their dial numbers.

Location of ethnic neighborhoods.

Copy of United States International Postal Regulations dealing with mailing letters and packages abroad.

(Regulations can be obtained by writing for "International Mail Regulations" to Publications Division, U.S. Post Office Department, Washington, D.C. 20260.)

List of cab drivers who speak foreign languages.

Theatre, ballet and opera information.

Local banks and brokers dealing in foreign currency exchange.

Giving Out Information About Guests

In smaller properties, the clerk, acting as the telephone operator, receives many calls asking if particular guests are in. Suppose the clerk knows Mr. X is not in but knows where he is; should the information be volunteered? Probably not. Should he/she inform Mr. X when he returns that he had a call? Probably not, unless he/she is prepared to tell Mr. X who called and the caller's phone number. Guests may get very upset when messages for them are garbled or incorrect.

In taking messages, repeat the message to the caller to ensure that it has been received perfectly clearly. Place the guest's message light on "message waiting." Then time stamp the receipt and delivery time of the message. Remember that, for want of the properly delivered message — the "contract *can be* lost."

Don't divulge room numbers of guests for security reasons. Simply refer the guest to a house phone so that the operator can ring the guest's room. If the inquiry comes by outside phone, connect the call to the room but do not state the room number.

And, as a security procedure, always verify the guest's name against the "room rack" before giving out a guest room key.

The Little Extras

Many things can be done at little or no cost. While every guest is not likely to be escorted by an assistant manager to the room, he or she can be made quite welcome by being called by name by the desk personnel and by the bellperson. As a matter of policy, everyone should make a habit of calling the guest by name at least once or twice during their contact with the person. This is an excellent way to make the guest feel important and at home.

Some other little extras that go a long way:

— Offer to make restaurant reservations for the guest.

— Tell the guest "Let me check the hold mail for messages or mail."

— Reassure the guest about his or her selection of rooms by stating something like, "I know you're going to enjoy this room, Ms. X."

— "If you need anything else, Mr. X, please call. I'd be happy to help you."

— "Have a nice stay."

— "May I give the operator your wake-up call time?"

— "Room service is open now if you'd like to place your breakfast order."

Depending upon hotel policy, front desk personnel may take the initiative in making the check-in/check-out procedure an overture to friendship. After a few visits to a hotel, the clerk and the guest develop a warmth of feeling so that both are pleased to see each other. In smaller properties, such relationships can develop into lasting friendships. The clerk, however, must take care in not favoring one guest over another when several are waiting for service. The stranger feels even more alone upon Jack Jovial being welcomed like Long Lost Brother while he gets the deadpan "Do you have a reservation?" treatment.

Follow-Up Calls

Some hotels have a policy of having the clerk call the guest room after 10 or 15 minutes of the person's being roomed and asking if everything is all right. Often a guest cannot figure out how to turn on the TV; the room may be too cold or too warm; he or she wants to know the hours of service for the dining room, etc., but hesitates to ask because of timidity or fear of appearing ignorant. The follow-up call is especially appreciated by female guests and should be made by a woman to a woman. It should be noted that few large hotels practice the follow-up call procedure.

Protecting Female, Elderly, and Disabled Guests

When there is a question of one area in a hotel or motel being safer than another, be sure to place female guests, elderly guests and disabled guests traveling alone in the best lighted and most secure section of the property.

A motel, part of a large chain, was the scene of a rape of a well-known entertainer. The intruder broke into her room, raped and robbed her. Suit was brought against the company on the grounds that the security and locks at the motel were defective and that this allowed the intruder to gain access to her room.

A New York jury awarded the woman damages in excess of $2,000,000 (later reduced to over $1,000,000). This action caused hotel operators to be much more careful as to where women traveling alone are roomed and about security measures taken to ensure their safety.

As said before, many hotels have a practice of making a follow-up call to all guests as a matter of courtesy. This would seem particularly appropriate for lone woman guests, elderly guests and disabled guests as a matter of reassurance and as an extension of friendship. The follow-up call could be rather routine:

"Good evening, Ms. Smith. This is Jane Bly at the front desk. I am just calling to see if everything is all right and if there is anything we can do for you."

Imperturbability

It's great to be called "imperturbable," especially in the hotel business. That adjective applied to a person means that he or she has the gift of remaining calm in the face of problems. Hemingway put it another way: "grace under stress." Keeping cool. Keeping a check-rein on emotions so that they can be used as a controlled engine rather than as a runaway train. Appearing imperturbable (whether you are or not) is a great asset.

Self-composure is a beautiful garb to be worn on all occasions at the front desk. Some diplomats are said to be "unflappable," a rare quality of maintaining their emotional equilibrium under trying conditions.

Act as though you are in control (even though you may not be). Try not to appear harried or overly hurried. In other words, don't act rushed unless the occasion calls for it.

Self-Composure

Maintaining one's composure is often a matter of appearance. A London maitre d'hotel who always seemed to be without a worry was asked how he did it. His reply: "I'm like a duck you see sailing serenely over a pond. On the surface I'm completely calm. Underneath I'm paddling like crazy."

Under the pressures that accumulate in guest relations, it is easy to lose self-composure, and to no avail. It helps not a bit to become overexcited, and it can be downright horrendous if panic sets in. Panic is like wildfire. It spreads. Guests may commiserate. They may understand. They may sympathize. But they lose respect for you. Tired, easily disturbed guests pick up the panic and run with it. They get more excited, even hysterical.

One manager of a large hotel has a solution. Whenever the pressures build up he, who is a transcendental meditation student, turns on his "mantra." He repeats a phrase to himself and quickly the tensions fade away. He is able to look more objectively at things. Psychologists recommend saying to yourself "Slow down. Slow down. Slow down." Relaxation is the goal, and it is accomplished differently by different people. A walk around the block may help. Swimming or other sports activity is a universal unraveler of the mind.

Any technique that reduces anxieties and tensions so as to avoid panic is worth considering.

At times, a thick skin is needed to take abuse that is not due, and it is easy to become defensive. The employee may also be forced into a position of taking on the burden of defending other members of the staff as the guest denounces "you people," "your establishment." If possible, do not take denunciations of "you" or "your" establishment personally. (Easier said than done, to be sure.)

Accepting Compliments Gracefully

Accepting compliments gracefully is a part of guest relations. How do we define "gracefully"? "Thank you very much" will do nicely. No need to be effusive in appreciation and no need to say that you do not deserve the praise. Better to accept the compliment quietly and without fanfare.

If other people deserve to be included in the compliment, the reply might include them as well: "All of us involved appreciate what you have said." Specific people should be included. You might want to add: "I will pass along your compliment to Ms. Smith and the others involved."

Guest Manipulation — a Definite No-No

Knowing something of guest psychology does not mean that we are justified in manipulating that person for our own or the hotel's benefit. Manipulation of people means maneuvering, or even deceiving them into feeling or doing something that is to the manipulator's advantage. Is a sweet hello a way of softening up the guest or of expressing good will? Deception often backfires and violates the employee's integrity. The tactful person can make a negative point honestly by indirection or silence. Guest relations avoids manipulation and benefits the guest. At the same time, it also benefits the employee and the hotel.

Avoid conversation about controversial subjects such as politics or religion. Nothing is gained by arguing or making counterstatements about any subject raised by a guest. If a guest insists on pursuing the subject, the employee can excuse him/herself or merely listen noncommittally.

Power and its Use

The desk clerk/receptionist has power at times: power to please, power to put down, power to assign superior rooms or inferior ones, and, on some occasions, power to provide or not provide a room. The clerk has power to expedite requests or to hold them up. Whenever anybody wants something from another — and the guest often wants something from the clerk — the person being asked assumes power. That person can take advantage of that power, and often does. The unscrupulous clerk may seek obsequiousness, little favors, or even money in the form of a bribe. The clerk may show his/her "power" by feigning indifference, holding up the registration process, acting disdainful or inattentive. No self-respecting room clerk will stoop to or indulge him or herself in such behavior.

A travel-worn person may be disoriented and lack confidence; some clerks attempt to be brusque and to talk down to such persons. Later, when these same guests are fresh and self-confident, these same clerks become obsequious.

It is not uncommon, especially in foreign countries, for room clerks to set themselves up in private business, taking advantage of their position to extract tips, and more despicably, bribes. Many travelers have found that even though the hotel is full, suddenly there is one room available if the clerk is slipped a five or ten-dollar bill. In busy locations, sometimes a network of clerks funnel guests from one property to another, provided the guest is ready to provide the proper gratuity. Of course, such behavior is outside the hotel policy, good taste, good manners and honest behavior. Be helpful, but don't hustle. Maintain your own sense of decency and pride, feelings which emanate from you to co-workers and to guests.

Put the Computer in Its Place

The computer can be seen as a device for providing more service, more quickly, more efficiently and with less chance of error. The clerk controls the computer — not vice versa — and should strive to give the impression that the computer is an instrument for providing more personal attention and better service.

Hotel critics are quick to complain that many modern hotels and motels are too standardized, too commercialized, too impersonal and cold. Efficient, yes, but hotels tend to look alike and the guest wakes up in his/her room wondering whether he/she is in Denver, Chicago or Florida. With the use of computers in hotels, the critic says he/she is now being processed like a commodity, taken in at the front desk, shunted to a room, fed a non-aesthetic meal and having money extracted on the way out.

If the front desk personnel relate to themselves and to the computer more than they do to the guest, that person has every right to feel dehumanized and to complain. Clerks sometimes fiddle with the computer and make comments about its effectiveness, or lack of it, while leaving the guest standing as a spectator to this byplay.

In reality, use of the computer can permit more time to be spent relating to the guest, less time on paperwork and making corrections.

Computers permit much faster registration of guests, sometimes in less than 30 seconds per guest. Room availability information is fed into the computer by housekeeping personnel and the clerk need only press a button to learn what rooms are available, out of order (O.O.O.) or on change. The clerk is spared considerable paperwork, and, at least theoretically, the clerk has more time to attend the guest, to answer questions and to treat him/her as an individual rather than as someone to be processed in and out of the hotel.

The computer then becomes what it is — a data processing tool to expedite front office procedures. The clerk should never get absorbed with the computer, comment about it to the guest, or act in any way as though the computer is an animate object.

Never say, "The computer has done it again."

"The computer will do everything for us."

"I'll ask the computer."

Such comments may be taken to suggest that the computer is more important than the guest. The impression may be that the computer is running things, not the clerk, not the management, that somehow the computer takes over and depersonalizes guest information.

Actually, the computer can be an asset to the guest. The instant a guest registers at the front desk, that information is stored and available to telephone operators, even before the guest reaches the room.

Any charges that a guest makes in a hotel restaurant can be immediately entered into the computer and added to his/her folio charges, which enables a speedy checkout.

Telephone operators, by locating guests' phone numbers more quickly by use of the computer, can expedite calls.

Depending upon the size of the computer, reservations can be stored in its memory for years in advance. Large computers can store past transitions for a number of years as well.

CHAPTER 4

SPECIAL INDUSTRY PROBLEMS

Many of the subjects mentioned thus far have had general guest relations application to the "service employee" in almost any service industry. This chapter deals with specific problems that might be encountered in the hotel or hospitality industry.

Overbooking and Walking the Guest

Management has failed to make an accurate count on departures and arrivals and expects a certain percentage of no-show reservations. About 10:00 P.M., the late evening count is made. There are 12 reservations and three rooms available. Within an hour the rooms are sold.

At 11:30 P.M., Mr. James Smith, president of a sizable manufacturing company, arrives and says, "Good evening. My name is James Smith; I have a reservation." The receptionist responds, "Mr. Smith, I'm sorry, but we don't have any rooms available."

In thinking out your response, keep in mind that it does not pay to be defensive with the customer. Be sincere, polite and genuine. Explain to the person that you will at once seek accommodations at a nearby property and that complimentary transportation will be made available (if indeed it will).

Also tell the guest (if it is house policy) that you will try to arrange to have him or her back in your hotel as soon as possible and that again transportation will be arranged.

You've been polite, understanding and apologetic. You've done everything possible. Don't dwell on the incident.

Some hotels are often overbooked by anywhere from 5 to 25 percent. Although it may be a company policy not to over-book, due to scheduled departures that did not leave, or guest rooms becoming out of order, hotels can "find themselves overbooked." This means that inevitably at times guests with confirmed reservations will get no room. The clerk/receptionist in such a situation is damned no matter what action is taken, even though he or she as an individual had no part in creating the situation. The irate guest must be mollified as much as possible and another room secured for him or her at another property or even in a home if necessary. If the clerk/receptionist is overly solicitous, an aggressive guest may take it as a sign to browbeat the receptionist, or as an opening to secure a room which he/she is certain has been held back by management.

Few things are more distracting or unpleasant for the clerk/receptionist and others in the vicinity than to have a "walked" guest on the rampage. Some aggressive types put on virtuoso performances; clerks have been physically assaulted and, in at least one instance in Latin America, been thrown in jail by a powerful VIP denied a room. In another instance, a Brazilian general was ordered out of a bar because of drunken behavior. He returned with a revolver vowing to kill the manager. (He didn't.)

PART II of this book treats the subject of overbooking and "walking" a guest in terms of how the clerk/receptionist can deal with the "game" the walked guest is inclined to play.

Hold Out Rewards

Whenever a guest is walked, and whatever the hotel policy about it, there is a residual negative effect — inconvenience to the guests at the very least. Some hotels and chains have poli-cies; if so, they should be explained at once, systematically and in a straightforward manner:

"I've arranged for a room at Hotel X at no charge to you and a cab is waiting outside to take you to that hotel, our compliments. Just as soon as possible we will have you back in our hotel in a premium room."

Westin Hotels International, for example, has such a policy, and also sees to it that the walked guest has a bottle of wine or a fruit basket in the room when the guest can be brought back to the hotel. If the guest is paying for the room from his/her own money, the offer of the free room may be reward enough. Those who are traveling on an expense account probably care very little about the free room at another hotel and are inevitably upset by the waste of time and inconvenience caused by being walked. The clerk should do his/her best to make the best of a bad situation, expressing sympathy and concern, reducing inconvenience to a minimum and making amends according to house policy.

Rooms out of order present a somewhat similar situation, an inconvenience to the guest at the very least. House policy in many hotels is to suggest, "Perhaps you would like to have a cup of coffee in our coffee shop, our compliments, while you are waiting."

Other hotels provide a complimentary drink at the bar if the room is out of order in the late afternoon or evening.

Prostitution

The clerk is not the face of public morality, but must be aware of the ambiguous standards regarding sex in the hotel, particularly regarding prostitution and its impact on a hotel.

When prostitution is obvious in a hotel (open solicitation for sexual favor in a public place), many guests otherwise inclined tend to downgrade the property at once.

Oddly enough, public figures of the Western world maintain a public stance against prostitution but sometimes buy the services of prostitutes and call girls, and some expect to engage in the practice in leading hotels. Public morality and reality, therefore, seem miles apart. The hotel manager is left in a dilemma. The manager is expected to eliminate prostitution in his/her property but knows that it is an expected service by many guests. Perhaps he/she should follow the example of the British aristocracy, who are quite comfortable with adultery and prostitution as long as it is done circumspectly. Maintain appearances. Society closes ranks to ostracize prostitutes and the hotel which openly permits or encourages prostitution may find itself on the skids.

Without moralizing further on the issue, the facts are: that every State in the United States has laws against prostitution. And, it is illegal in every State in the United States for an innkeeper to knowingly rent a room for an illegal purpose. Such action lays the innkeeper open to the misdemeanor charge of "operating a disorderly house." Some hotels or motels advertise porno movies and mirrored ceilings; the better hotels act as though sex doesn't exist.

This writer is of the opinion that there is a strong obligation to protect the reputation of the hotel and as a result, act to prevent prostitution from occurring through open solicitation in the public areas of the hotel. However, when a stylishly dressed person whom you think you have seen before, enters the hotel, passes through the lobby, enters an elevator, proceeds to a guestroom, knocks on a door and is allowed to enter that room by the person inside the room; stay out of it. That may be someone's wife or daughter . . . or son.

Some Things Better Left Unnoticed

It may be too much to ask of anyone to close his or her ears and eyes to scandal and the many foibles of human nature to which the clerk/receptionist may become privy. When a man checks into the hotel, soon followed by a woman who requests the room next door, or vice versa, it takes no great imagination to suspect a liaison. The policy of most hotels is to stay out of guests' personal business unless it affects the good name of the hotel. The clerk becomes concerned when such behavior becomes so obvious that it creates an untoward image of the hotel. The room clerk calls the attention of the security officer to obvious solicitation or "traffic" in and out of a room or, if necessary, calls the manager, depending upon house policy.

Be very clear with employees about the house policy and sex.

The Wrong Room Key

Another situation which occurs once in a while: The guest is given the key to the wrong room in a hotel. He/she comes back and gets another key. Sometimes even this key does not work because the locks have been changed or the lock does not open easily. The clerk who gave the wrong key may not be on duty or may be busy elsewhere. Another clerk faces the problem. Whoever the clerk, he or she should apologize sincerely and go with the guest to the room with the master key if necessary.

Guests can be expected sometimes to be unreasonable, but from their viewpoint, perfectly responsible and justified in flaring up at an inconvenience or delay. Guests coming in from flights often have their luggage lost by the airlines, the flight may have been several hours late, the traffic on the way to the hotel may have been bumper to bumper. The guest indeed needs sympathy, and ordinarily will deeply appreciate sincere concern for his/her welfare. In PART II, the subject of "Stroking" will deal with this issue.

The Advance Payment Problem

The receptionist may not agree with certain house polices, but must live with them nevertheless and try to understand the reasons for such policies. Sometimes it is difficult to explain a house policy to a guest. Even so it must be done without any suggestion that the policy can be relaxed. A case in point:

Many hotels have a policy that if a guest has "a same day reservation," is a "walk in" and is not carrying a standard credit card, he/she must pay with cash. The same holds true for a guest without any luggage, even though the luggage may have been lost in flight. The guest often takes umbrage at such a policy, interpreting it as a reflection on his/her personal honesty. When a guest cannot be placated, refer that person to the manager or other supervisor. This keeps the desk area organized and maintains a pleasant atmosphere while satisfying the ego of the guest.

If the guest is tired or has had a couple of drinks, the time and care in making the explanation may be extended. People who are tired or inebriated think slowly and are apt to be on the defensive. They may also appreciate a sympathetic ear much more than when at their best.

Narrow the Choices

Most hotels require that the guest establish credit before being roomed. This can present a real problem in that some guests do not use credit cards. Any suggestion that they establish credit is taken as an affront, an implication that their credit is not good. A standard question narrows the choice given the guest and partly avoids raising the question of honesty. The clerk asks, "Will you be paying by credit card or with cash in advance?" The question suggests that these are the only two alternatives, even though there may be other choices. Another alternative: "Would you like to establish credit with us, or will you be paying cash in advance?"

When the guest announces that he or she carries no credit cards and has never paid cash in a hotel before, the clerk may have no option but to refer the person to an assistant manager or credit manager, but to do so in the most gracious manner possible: "Would you mind following me to meet Ms. Jones, our credit manager, who can help you arrange credit here?"

More on this will be covered in the next section, where transactional analysis is applied to the same problem.

House policy establishes the maximum amount of money which can be had by cashing a check, and this, too, may cause inconvenience to a guest, particularly foreigners who must be referred to a bank and who must show their passports in order to have travelers' checks in large amounts cashed. Verification of credit with a bank can be done in a day by calling the guest's bank, but this is often impossible if the guest stays but one night or during weekends when banks are closed. There is little recourse for the hotel but to refuse to room the person or to accept a check which may bounce.

The Overcharge Complaint

There are times when guests are overcharged for one reason or another. Sometimes the guest feels that it is not a mistake, but that he or she has been discriminated against. One such instance occurred when a cashier was checking out a group of men and one of them questioned the reason he was being charged at a higher rate than his friends. Everyone had received the corporate rate except him. He was paying a rate of about one-third more. As it turned out, the overcharged guest had not made a reservation as part of the corporate group and so was not given the corporate rate. The guest proved that he was an employee of the same company by presenting a business card and his folio was adjusted accordingly.

It could be argued that the guest who complained about his rate should not have had his bill adjusted because the guest did not follow proper procedures. Unfortunately, this attitude is too easy to adopt. It takes objective thinking in solving charge problems such as these. Sometimes the best way to view the problem is to put yourself in the guest's place.

In disputes over charges, especially those dealing with phone charges, many hotels have a policy of taking the guest's word rather than arguing over a few dollars and losing the guest forever. Other house policies require the guest be referred to an assistant manager or manager. Phone charges are one of the touchiest of subjects because the guest may have forgotten that certain calls were made. The calls may have been made by a roommate, or indeed there may have been mistaken charges made by the operators, or by someone in another room making charges against the wrong room.

It should be remembered that, if there is a difference of a dollar or so, writing letters to collect such a small sum can cost more than the amount owed. That, however, is a matter for the management to decide.

Lost Laundry

Problem situation: The guest approaches the front desk and explains that the laundry and dry cleaning sent out the day before has not been returned. The clerk follows the standard procedure established by the hotel in backtracking the laundry and checks with the bellperson or the person who collected the laundry. That person checks with the laundry hold/storage and reports back that the laundry is not there.

The receptionist then contacts the laundry itself (whether it is in-house or out-of-house). The laundry confirms that the particular guest's laundry has been received and returned.

(In the instance cited, the laundry had been inadvertently delivered to another hotel). But the guest is checking out immediately.

The guest may demand to be reimbursed, in which case it becomes the management's problem.

The bellperson may have been negligent in not checking the laundry list against actual delivery. The laundry, too, was in error.

The receptionist should immediately apologize for what has happened and ask the guest if the laundry can be forwarded to an address of the guest's choice (sometimes the guest may not want the laundry sent home).

The receptionist has been sincerely concerned over the guest's problem and has acted immediately to learn what happened to the laundry. The guest has observed this concern and probably will appreciate the action taken. Ordinarily, the laundry can be forwarded the next day to the address of the guest's choice.

Ellsworth M. Statler, one of the most successful and adept hoteliers in history, had a policy of never arguing over small amounts. If a guest had a shirt torn in the laundry, there was no question but of paying the guest the cost of a new shirt. If the guest said that he or she had lost anything or had been overcharged, an adjustment was made immediately and with apology.

Prompt attention to any guest complaint which is at all reasonable makes friends for the hotel and shows the guest that the hotel personnel really are concerned and care about the guest's well-being and satisfaction. Any complaint must be taken seriously, the clerk paying close attention to what is said and showing concern. To paraphrase Gertrude Stein, who liked to repeat things for emphasis, "A guest is a guest, is a guest, is a guest." Somewhere there is a fine line. Of course, a well-mannered guest in a private home would never complain about anything. A hotel guest is expected to have justifiable complaints. They should never be taken as a personal affront by the clerk any more than a physician should immerse him or herself in sorrow over a patient who does not recover.

Handling Emergencies

The best psychology for handling any emergency is to be prepared. "Be forehanded" as the Navy says. The value of experience and training is that "You've been through it before." Even the courts are holding innkeepers liable for reasonable caution and precaution in cases where foreseeability is indicated. Even so, there is always the unexpected. C. DeWitt Coffman relates a number of them in his book *Keyhole Insights*.[1]

A drunk claimed he had been bitten in a hotel room; the house officer proved he had sat down hard on his own dentures.

A woman took down the guest room drapes, made herself a nice dress of them and, after she checked out, walked out wearing the dress.

Then there are the obvious Romeos and their dates who come into the hotel acting quite sedate, register as husband and wife and demand a three-hour room rate.

Some guests have been known to drop water bombs on pedestrians in the street not knowing that, after a 20-or 30-floor fall, a water bomb can be a deadly weapon. Lamps have been dropped out of windows just to hear them break.

An entertainment group claimed they had no connecting door to the next room. They took a fire ax from the hall and made their own door . . . Voila, a door.

A pedestrian charged into a Miami Beach hotel lobby saying he had been hit by a frozen turkey thrown from a window. It turned out the employees had a good thing going by tossing turkeys from the second floor to accomplices below. One turkey had been misdirected.

Guests can be expected to do almost anything. A guest lacerated his head as he butted the screen on the television set in his room while watching a professional football game.

Those known as "professional divers" fake accidents and collect insurance.

Every restaurant operator is supposed to know what to do when a guest chokes on a piece of food lodged in the throat. At the old Savoy Plaza in New York City a sheik from a Middle Eastern nation had just such a predicament. The house doctor tried the usual methods and determined that only a tracheotomy would save him. When he tried to use the scalpel for the necessary throat incision, the sheik's aides threw the physician to the floor and threatened his life. The sheik died.

Guests have been known to smash their fists while attacking a burglar who turned out to be themselves reflected in the mirror.

House policy should establish routines for various kinds of

emergencies:

What to do in case of robbery.

What to do in case of fire.

What to do in case of fighting in the lobby.

What to do in case of a bomb threat.

Whatever the emergency, the clerk/receptionist who keeps his or her cool is ahead of the game. Never try to be a hero. Let the professionals do what they are being paid to do.

When a Guest Steals

For some reason, many hotels guests think nothing of walking off with hotel property. Taking a guest towel may not be considered stealing at all. "We're only collecting souvenirs." Guests have been known to take anything that is movable — sheets, blankets, pillowcases; yes, TV sets. That is why pictures and TV sets are bolted to walls and heavy furniture.

When the housekeeping department or security people have reason to suspect that the guest is checking out with hotel property, they call the front desk. In some hotels, and especially motels, the clerk then has the unenviable task of confronting the guest with what amounts to an accusation.

Be sure to know the house policy in such a situation. Since lawsuits have become so popular, house policy is often "to forget the whole thing." Lawsuits take time and cost money. They can also prove highly embarrassing, especially if the guest is proven innocent. The policy of many hotels is to simply overlook small thefts — a towel, a sheet or an ashtray.

If the policy is to confront a guest suspected of stealing, keep calm and speak in a low voice. Because of embarrassment for all concerned if the conversation is overheard by other guests, speak to the guest privately. A member of management asks the guest into the manager's office and invites the guest to open his or her suitcase. The usual ploy goes like this:

"Pardon me, Mr. Smith, it has been suggested that you may have accidentally placed hotel property in your bag. Would you mind stepping into the manager's office with me?" Sometimes the threat of calling the police brings forth the stolen property.

The "accidentally" gives the guest a chance to save face and return the property quietly and without fuss. If indeed the guest is innocent, there will probably be no hesitation in opening his or her bag to prove that nothing in it belongs to the hotel.

Some managers simply bill the guest for anything missing from the room if fairly certain the guest is guilty.

It has happened that items reported missing have actually been taken by employees (a tactic to allay suspicion.)

In any event, it does the hotel's reputation no good to have it bruited about that the guests were caught red-handed while checking out with hotel property.

Keep it quiet, keep calm and do the best you can without causing a furor.

That "Old Tender Loving Care"

To conclude this chapter, this is some of what James M. Kilpatrick, nationally syndicated columnist, had to say about room clerks and front desk operations: "All that the traveling man really wants on the road is a little tender loving care and it seems to be hard to come by . . . the operative word is 'care.' Those of us who spend much of our lives at the mercy of desk clerks want someone to care if we are comfortable. We want someone, somewhere in the hostelry, to care a whole lot. Here and there one encounters the old TLC, but the here-and-theres get fewer all the time." Tender loving care is also a social lubricant, facilitating interpersonal relations.

Another way of saying the same thing is, "How about a little empathy?" Empathy means putting yourself into the skin of the other person. Put yourself in the place of the guest and imagine how the guest feels. Coming off the highway after driving all day, or arriving at the hotel after a long flight, the guest is obviously tired.

The guest may say, "My flight was delayed for three hours."

The emphathetic desk clerk/receptionist can respond, "You must be exhausted." The receptionist cares. Empathy: "identifying" with the other person.

ENDNOTES

1. Coffman, DeWitt C., *Keyhole Inn-sights: An Uninhibited Peek Into the Hotel World*, (New York), Prentice-Hall, 1972.

CHAPTER 5

COMMUNICATION IN OTHER FORMS

ON THE TELEPHONE

The telephone can be seen as an enemy or as an extension of the personality, a fantastic technical device multiplying the individual's effectiveness. Like Pavlov's dog, one becomes conditioned to the phone's ring. Instead of salivating, one can react with more adrenalin or calm. The phone ring can be an irritant or it can be a challenge to expedite, serve and create good will. Like any useful tool, one should learn to use it well. The voice is the medium. There is nothing else, however, no gestures, no props in this play. Not even telepathy to help carry the message.

Telephone Techniques

Telephone companies and other companies have produced a set of guidelines for talking on the phone — guidelines that, when followed, help to create a favorable impression for the telephone user that makes the telephone a fantastic, imaginary bridge between caller and called:

1. Maintain a reference file of often-used numbers. The file may be nothing more than a small notebook separated alphabetically, or it may be a set of code cards which, when fed into specialized equipment, dial the number on the card automatically.

2. For long distance calls, it is usually faster to dial the area information service than to go through the operator.

3. Plan long distance calls to take advantage of lower rates. This means that a person calling the East Coast from the West Coast can call at 7 o'clock in the morning and get the East Coast party at 10 A.M. Eastern time. In making long distance calls, avoid the called party's mealtimes.

4. Plan what is to be said before calling. This may mean making notes and checking them off as the call proceeds.

5. If needed information is not at hand and it would take longer than a minute to look it up, it is better to call the person back.

6. Speak distinctly into the phone. Do not speak loudly; try to keep a pleasant modulation to avoid sounding like a talking machine.

7. Personalize phone conversations by using the other person's name once or twice in the conversation - this can be overdone, but most people enjoy hearing their name used.

8. In answering the phone:

— Put a smile in the voice - or at least some spirit and warmth.

— Act as though the person were attractive and you were face-to-face. Within reason, respond to the mood of the caller.

— Be prompt; answer as soon as possible, ordinarily within three rings. Put the caller on "hold" only as a last resort and only after establishing the caller's priority.*

— Greet the caller pleasantly; make him or her feel that you are pleased to receive the call.

— Give the caller your undivided attention — a form of courtesy that suggests you are businesslike and can concentrate.

— Allow the caller to hang up first, if possible. Again, a matter of courtesy.

— Always identify the department when answering the phone. Many businesses have a policy of saying,

"Good morning," "Good afternoon" or Good evening," as the case may be.

— When ending a call, recap all the arrangements or agreements, if necessary, and end the conversation by using the caller's name and some phrase such as "Thank you for calling."

9. Remember, the voice on the phone — your voice — is the voice of the business.

10. Always take the caller's phone number so if the line is disconnected you can call back.

Avoid Transferring Calls Unless Necessary

What can be more exasperating to a caller than being transferred about and often left hanging on the line? Even more frustrating, is for the call to be lost and the caller forced to start the call over again. It is courteous to ask, "Will you wait?" or, "Shall I call back?"

If it takes longer than anticipated to gather the material or to find an answer, the caller should be assured every 30 seconds that work is progressing on the request. Progress reports let the caller know something is being done and create understanding.

When a transfer is made, the call should be identified to the transferee to prepare the person for the call and to avoid having the caller repeat the information already given.

Take Complete Messages

Spell the name of the person completely, as well as the company represented. Repeat the message to see if it has been taken down correctly. And don't forget the telephone number. Make a note of the information required. Note the time the call was received.

End on an upbeat. The calling party receives a feeling of satisfaction if the conversation is brought to a natural close and the person thanked. Again, try to allow the caller to hang up first.

Selling by Phone

Selling by phone leaves the salesperson completely dependent upon verbal communication. Body language such as nodding, eye contact and hand gestures cannot be seen and used as non-verbal communication. The voice and its use is paramount.

Time is limited: the words and the approach must be right. The phone salesperson cannot pick up the usual cues coming from the prospect. Reactions must be guessed. The salesperson usually has one choice of approach because of time limitations. A mistake in approach and the sale is lost. The salesperson must rely on the prospect's tone of voice and pauses in response.

The salesperson should carefully outline what will be covered in the sales pitch. To successfully sell by phone requires a pleasant and distinct tone. Avoid the monotone, the "canned" speech. Use word pictures where possible. Describe whatever is being sold in descriptive terms. In selling a hotel, for example, sell the olympic-sized pool, the cabanas, the beach, the queen-sized beds, the view, the meeting rooms. Tell the prospect what the product will do for him or her. Be polite, cheerful and enthusiastic.

Try to close the sale. Be very clear on what will happen next. "I'll call you tomorrow if that's convenient." "You can reach me at 598-4918." "Do I have your permission to call Mr. Big and tell him that we have talked?" "The contract will be in the mail this afternoon."

Some DO's and DON'Ts

DO SAY	DON'T SAY
Front office, Ms. Jones speaking, may I help you?	Ms. Jones speaking.
I'm sorry that the $20 rooms are completely sold, but we do have lovely $24 rooms left.	No, we are sold out of $20 rooms.
We can offer you . . .	I can offer you . . .
May I make a reservation for you?	Do you want a reservation?
Thank you for calling the Palace Hotel.	Thanks for calling.
Thank you for waiting.	Hello, are you there?
Please wait while I get the information for you.	Just a minute.
Yes, thank you.	Okay.
We have a beautiful room on the 20th floor.	I can give you a room on the 20th floor.
May I be of service?	What can I do for you?
May I tell him who is calling?	Who's calling?

Some telephone companies are pleased to send a trainer into a hotel and offer a telephone techniques training course at no charge to the hotel. Such courses involve training films, roleplaying and practice sessions critiqued by front desk personnel, sales personnel and other guest contract employees, including the manager's secretary.

NONVERBAL COMMUNICATION

Good actors are well aware of the effect of posture, voice level and the multitude of gestures and gesticulations that go together to project the assigned role. Guest-contact employees can be more effective knowing something about what has come to be known as nonverbal communication, how to better portray their roles and read what others are saying without words.

How often have you heard, "We just don't communicate," or "It's a problem in communication." To communicate, says Webster, is "to make known." How? Presumably by the spoken word, visual symbols, touch, pain, warmth, cold and other means. In guest relations, we tend to assume that we "make known" mostly by words and, perhaps, writing. But consider body language, touching and brushing, and those subconscious signals we receive that together form empathy, allowing us to feel what the customer is feeling.

Read the Body

The spoken language is the main vehicle of communication in face-to-face meetings. But what does the body tell us? The mouth may say one thing while the body sends another message. Reading the body may give us the real information. Every society fosters formal gestures that are often used to hide real feelings. Smiling with the lips only is such a gesture. Are the eyes crinkled with the opening of the mouth? Are the eyes laughing with the opening of the lips? Is the handshake firm and strong or is it merely a formality? Does the body say "I'm tense" while the lips say "I'm fine"?

Women tend to be superior to men in judging nonverbal communications. They notice the hand movements, the body posture, the tension expressed in the voice.

Many of the cues are subconsciously observed, the observer not really being aware of why he or she feels that the other person is friendly, not friendly, warm, excited, placid, merely being polite and so on.

Much can be learned from the tone of voice. Under emotion, voice pitch almost always changes. Nonverbal clues are also expressed — clues which may be more useful than what is said. For many people, the body does not know how to deceive. These nonverbal clues have been labeled "body language."

The body signals which accompany the words, the posture, the position of arms, hands and fingers, the tension expressed in the way the body is poised, or relaxed, say something also. Much can be read about a person's true feelings by the signals given off in "body language."

According to one author, "studies have shown that only 7 percent of face-to-face communication is accomplished by words. Vocal intonation and inflection account for 38 percent. Facial expression and body language account for 55 percent.[1] Such precise percentages are probably not possible, but certainly the way something is said - the enthusiasm, sincerity, force and so on - makes a great deal of difference in the way the message is received.

Interpretation of body stance and movement, however, can be overdone. Just as with the interpretation of dreams, any simple interpretation can be misleading. Body language enthusiasts are likely to be much too rigid in their interpretation of various behaviors. For example, women are said to be "more than available" if they twist or pull at their hair or sit with their legs apart. Pulling at one's hair can be a sign of nervousness and nothing else, and sitting with one's legs apart may mean that the person is relaxed.

So-called preening gestures such as adjusting one's tie, checking one's fingernails or adjusting one's socks may be more a sense of insecurity than preening as suggested by the body language enthusiasts.

The ability to read body language varies widely, but most of us respond to smiles one way, smirks another. Clenched fists are probably universally seen as threatening. Direct staring can be taken as threatening or as sexual interest.

Some behavior is obviously aggressive: scowling, shaking a fist, fingering the nose, finger pointing, throwing back the chest, hands on the hips or waving the arms.

Nervousness is difficult to mask. Fidgeting, eye blinking, tight lips, deep breathing, frequent shifting of weight from foot to foot or shifting one's chair can result from tension. Picking the nose, compulsive scratching, running a hand through the hair, jerky body movements or a strained voice all suggest tension on the muscular level.

Excitement, from whatever cause, dilates the pupils of the eyes, a reflex action which prepares the body for action. An abnormal amount of tongue movement may mean nervousness or lack of ease.

Frequent wetting of the lips suggests nervousness. The dry mouth reaction has been used by some primitive cultures to identify the guilty party in a crime. Elders of the tribe examine the mouths of suspects or require them to eat some dry food. The highly nervous person has difficulty in swallowing the food because of lack of saliva.

Because much of body language is learned behavior, it varies from one culture to another. Asians tend to smile when under stress; a person raised in the U.S. acts differently. Italians are known for their free and ready use of gestures. Lebanese crowd in on each other, gesticulate and raise their voices. Repeated eye contact may mean that the person has taken an assertion training course or a Dale Carnegie Course, or it may indeed be an indication of self-confidence and forcefulness; or the person is "gaze-holding" as a means of indicating sexual interest. Latins generally maintain more eye contact than North Americans. American Indians are thought to behave more stoically than Caucasians. Yet, in some tribes, it is perfectly acceptable for men to cry in public.

People often read too much into various positions and postures. They say that when a person touches his or her nose, strong doubt is being expressed. Touching the nose, they say, means "no." Touching the nose may be a sign of nervousness. The body language enthusiasts believe that when a woman touches her breasts or thighs or slowly moves her fingers, it is part of a courtship ritual. If the woman removes one shoe and dangles it on a toe of the foot, that, too, is part of the ritual. It may not be. Some general "body language":

1. A person hunched up, neck taut, body rigid is obviously under stress. The expression "he is a pain in the neck" may be literally true. The person causes the speaker to tense up. The result may be a pain in the neck from increased tension.

2. A person leaning forward toward a speaker is probably very interested in what the speaker says.

3. Dilated pupils mean excitement (or perhaps drugs).

4. Arms akimbo or stretched across the chest suggest a defensive position.

5. A finger pointed suggests an aggressive, emphatic position.

6. Arms waved up and down suggest strong emotion and perhaps aggression.

7. Slumping in a chair or leaning back in a chair while listening or speaking suggests relaxation, perhaps a loss of interest or a desire to move away from a speaker.

8. Raised or arched eyebrows suggest surprise and interest.

9. Yawning while listening may mean the person is fatigued or has lost interest.

10. Gazing away from a speaker might mean embarrassment or lack of interest, or may be the person's habitual way of relating to another person.

11. Tapping one's foot might be caused by nervousness, desire to be somewhere else or impatience.

Touching and Brushing

Brushing or touching a guest is a form of communication. Much of its significance is subliminal (below the conscious level). Research has shown that touching and holding is necessary for normal human development. Babies who are neither held nor have the opportunity to cling to another person can end up severely maladjusted. They may also experience physiological changes, including blood chemistry changes. Monkeys that have been isolated physically from their mothers exhibit severe behavior problems and even brain damage.

An experiment in which an attractive female bank teller brushed the hand of a number of customers while handing them their passbooks is instructive. Half of the customers were touched by the teller; half were not.

Immediately following the transaction between the teller and customer, the customers were asked to evaluate their feelings about the transactions. Even though many of the customers who were physically touched were unaware of the act, they reacted much more favorably to the transaction than those customers who were not touched. The fact that the teller was an attractive woman was probably important. Women as well as men, however, responded favorably to touching.

If a cashier or server is attractive, touching the guest is almost certain to cause a positive reaction in the average American guest. People highly sensitive to status may react unfavorably, unless the employee is especially attractive.

Touching and familiarity are related to status. Most people accept a pat, a hand on the shoulders or a grasp of the arm by someone respected. If the person making the gesture is seen as having higher status, the individual receiving the gesture usually responds favorably, and may be flattered by the familiarity. A similar gesture made by a person seen as having lower status could be deeply resented: "Who does this person think he or she is?"

Touching or brushing a patron can be highly positive — or highly negative, depending on the people involved.

Empathy in Action

Empathy, putting yourself in the other person's shoes, is partly an attitude. Some people are experts at understanding how the other person feels. Women seem to be better at picking up the little cues from others that signal:

"I'm tired."

"I'm elated!"

"I'm hurt."

"I'm overwhelmed."

"I need help."

"I need reassurance."

Tuning in on the customer increases the employees' emphathetic index and provides data for responding to the customer's needs - needs that are psychological as well as material.

As psychologists put it, there are times when people need "disclosure," a time to tell someone our problems, a time for a sympathetic ear. The guest-service employee is neither psychologist nor counselor. But it is possible to be a listener, at least for a brief time. The guest probably does not expect agreement. The guest most certainly wants understanding. At the very least, employees should nod and act as though they understand the feelings behind the words.

Head Nodding

Nodding the head when listening to a customer may suggest sympathy or, under some circumstances, commiseration. A series of slow head nods reinforces what is said by another. It may mean agreement, or merely "I understand." A series of fast head nods generally suggests that the listener wants to speak. It may mean, "I agree; I understand; now, let me talk."

The stiff-necked person is at a disadvantage in nonverbal communication. The speaker may be left wondering whether the listener is even slightly interested in what is said, especially if the listener fails to look at the speaker.

Head nodding, however, can create misunderstanding. The customer may interpret a head nod as complete agreement when it is only intended as "I hear you."

Communications in a Restaurant Setting

The restaurant patron enters a dinner house and is greeted, "Hi, how many?" Hardly the warm welcome expected. How much better when the host or hostess uses a modicum of imagination and says, "Good evening. Glad you could join us tonight." At least something is said that initiates a social interaction, not a simple interrogation, as in "How many?" or "May I have your name?"

The host/hostess is supposed to act, as the job title implies, as a host/hostess — welcoming the newly-arrived patron, saying a few kind words and acting as though one is really pleased to have the person pay the restaurant a visit. Like the hotel desk clerk/receptionist, the guest service employee is the first representative of the restaurant to come face-to-face with the customer. This person sets the tone for the dining experience.

The sweet, young man or woman who at first is thrilled with the guest relations job begins to get bored, and the press of business can easily turn him or her from being the outgoing, warm and friendly person next door into a traffic cop. "Leave your name and we'll call you" or "Sit over there until a table opens up." With fatigue, the big hello wears thin. The smile, if there at all, turns plastic. The employee may not recognize real job motivation.

What the host/hostess may really want is the opportunity to socialize and to meet new people, especially potential dates. If the host/hostess recognizes his/her real motivations, he/she may be more satisfied with the job.

The Programmed Host/Hostess

The host/hostess may be programmed, to say and do things that cause patrons to begin enjoying themselves. The host/hostess looks the patron full in the face, smiles and says: "Good evening, sir/madam. Welcome to OUR PLACE." Obviously, the patron wants common courtesy, which means recognition, respect and a friendly welcome. One of the reasons people dine out almost invariably includes the desire for sociability. Failing to meet this basic need is an unnecessary form of deprivation foisted on the customer by an unthinking service person. The service person has mixed up priorities.

The programmed host/hostesss wears an appropriate uniform for the establishment. A theme dinner house restaurant may want the host/hostess in a specific theme uniform, but most places set a tone by having the host/hostess well-dressed in a business or formal attire, even though table and drink servers may be in a more theme-oriented costume.

The good host/hostess works at maintaining a proper appearance, posture and overall personality, which means adequate rest, exercise and diet.

He or she knows the duties and responsibilities of all positions in the dining room so that he or she can help, when necessary, to set up tables or to clear them.

The host/hostess ensures that service stations are presentable at all times, checks on the general temperature of the dining room and its cleanliness and is knowledgeable about the menu and what goes into each item, especially the advertised specials.

He or she never takes advantage of a professional position to arrange a date or make personal phone calls on duty, except in emergencies.

Having knowledge about the cashiering function is important in order to help the cashier at checkout time if need be. He or she should be cool and poised in case of emergency, and should know the planned approach to each likely emergency.

Professional hosts/hostesses are aware of the general appearance of the restaurant, including the parking lot and its lighting.

Finally, he or she works at being charming without being obvious about it.

If a customer complains, the good host/hostess gives the person the courtesy of listening to the whole complaint. He or she should never make the person feel that their complaint is unimportant. Good guest service personnel are friendly and tell people that the management of the restaurant is glad the problem, "was called to our attention." Cancellation of charges or replacement of food is done according to house policy and the judgment of the manager.

The good host/hostess leaves the departing guest with a pleasant memory of the establishment by saying something appropriate, such as "Good-bye, we hope to see you again soon," or "Glad you could dine with us tonight."

Throughout the customer contact, the host/hostess, like all service personnel, tries to avoid sounding like a tape recording.

The skilled host/hostess knows women usually do not like being seated facing a wall. One restaurant operator puts it this way: "When you seat a woman dining with her husband so that she faces a wall, the chances are ten-to-one she'll have a quarrel with him before the dessert is served." The same notion applies to seating two couples at a banquette (fixed seating with a high back). Seat the ladies to face the room unless a different arrangement is preferred.

When a man and a woman are dining together and the server cannot determine who is the host, the check is placed at an equal distance between them.

The Servers

It is generally accepted that servers contribute as much to

University of Ulster LIBRARY

the dining experience, or perhaps more, than the decor, appointment, background music, lighting and even the food served. In studies of customer reactions to restaurants, the National Restaurant Association found "quality of service" ranked number one in number of compliments received, and also as the "most frequent complaint." Service was ranked ahead of food quality and price consideration. (Parking and traffic congestion came in for the most complaints after service.)

Customer service, including customer recognition, is important for all restaurants, but particularly so for dinner houses.

Bennigan's, a highly successful dinner house chain, has researched why customers stop coming to their restaurants. Their findings show that:

— 1% die.

— 3% move away.

— 5% form other friendships.

— 9% have competitive reasons.

— 15% cite product dissatisfaction.

— 67% quit coming because of the attitude of indifference toward them by some employee.

What better evidence of the value of customer relations?!

The psychology of waiting as practiced by the server, of course, varies tremendously with the type of food service establishment, from the hot dog emporium to the deluxe dinner house. The teenager at a fast food restaurant is probably thrilled with working as a part of a team of other teenagers in an air-conditioned, well-lighted, well-appointed and fast-paced establishment. The skills required are minimal: assembly of food orders, a few simple cooking skills, making change. Most important, though, is the customer contact and the pleasure in working with one's peers. Supervision is minimal; most of the motivation comes from the necessity of keeping up with customer demand.

Consider the more complex relationships and skills required in a dinner house. The dining area is usually broken up into tables and booths, the booths forming separate environments unto themselves. Each booth provides something of the territorial imperative, the walls visually blocking some stimuli and providing social distance from other patrons, facilitating social interaction among those seated within the booth. The booth can be thought of as providing social and psychological security while accentuating the need for interaction of the group participants. Group participants are physically forced to look at each other and focus attention on those sitting within the confines of the booth. Its very design establishes intimacy and makes for a more relaxed atmosphere.

The server standing at the head of the booth more easily commands the attention of those seated there and tends to interact with them as a group more than as individuals. Everyone hears what everyone else is saying, including what each orders. The server need not repeat answers to questions and can establish a rapport with the group as a group, answering questions, explaining the menu and making suggestions.

Single individuals entering a restaurant feel alone, outsiders as related to the couples and parties. If seated at exposed tables, they may feel even more isolated and uncomfortable. On the other hand, the host/hostess or maitre d' is reluctant to tie up a booth with a single. If the individual is noticeably shy or ill at ease, the decision should be for the booth. A Gallup Poll study found that solos appreciated and were made comfortable by fast, friendly service. They did not like sharing a table, nor did they want to be seated in a special section for singles. Men seemed to prefer more attention from servers, while added service disturbed some women. Wine by the glass was appreciated. More women than men said they like eating alone.

Servers can expect more problems with people seated in open space — more complaints about noisy people at neighboring tables, uneasiness, concern over speed of service and defensive behavior.

Banquet rooms can be expected to produce the same sort of customer behavior. Often the customer is seated next to someone he or she knows only casually, or not at all. It usually takes an aggressive, self-assured person to break the ice of separateness and to begin the formation of group feeling. Low lighting is favorable for the dinner house, encouraging people to relax and helping to break down social distance. In the fast-food establishment and in the coffee shop, the lighting is brighter, in keeping with the mood of the customer who wants to eat quickly and move on. In a darkened room, people are encouraged to speak and act more intimately and to focus on those in the party rather than on the distractions of people entering, leaving or moving around.

Role Playing

Service people often play charades with the customers: "the student working his way through college," "the attractive young girl who might be your daughter" and "the old family retainer" are typical. The waiter/server-customer relations could well be a one-act play, with an opening, a plot development and a denouement. A customer is greeted as the play opens; as the meal progresses, the drama proceeds; the check is presented, the bill paid and the curtain goes down.

Many servers are skilled performers in the waiting role. The dinner house and, especially the lounge, is the stage. The server and the customer are both actors in the play. Both knowingly engage in the drama. The payoff for the customer is the feeling of warmth, friendship and ego enhancement. The reward for the server is the big tip and the excitement of the drama.

With some service people, the play is the thing. They know

103

they are acting and love it. They may also "love" their customers. The customers feed back similar feelings, a staged love affair. All smiles and attention, the waiter/waitress hangs on the customer's every word and gesture, radiating good will and the desire to please. The college-age server reminds the older woman of her son or daughter. Instant affection and good will result.

Once the meal is finished, the play is over, the customer leaves and the server moves on to the next stage. Should the customer and the server meet in the supermarket the next morning, they scarcely acknowledge each other. (The same thing may happen on a plane trip — the flight attendant dispenses love and warmth in flight, but off the plane, the play is over. Should a passenger pass the flight attendant in the terminal, they scarcely nod in recognition.)

The dinner house adds liquor to the environment, loosening inhibitions, enveloping the imbiber, clouding perceptions and, hopefully, reducing anxieties and hostilities. Voices rise, suppressed needs surface, conversations become animated, ego guards are lowered, jokes are funnier and all of a sudden the server turns into an interesting individual with a private life.

Psychological purse strings are loosened and the bottle of wine that at $12 seemed too expensive becomes a necessary part of having a decent meal. The servers become more intimate, may touch the customer on the arm or brush him/her in going by. Currents of good will flow.

The traveling person eating alone may be uneasy, especially in a dinner house where couples and groups are out having fun. Alienated and self-conscious, he or she may wonder about the price of the meal and may order something more expensive than ordinarily ordered to let anyone who might be interested know that the meal was affordable. The traveler may want more rapid service, eating quickly and leaving as soon as possible. This does not mean that the server should assume that every lone traveler is uneasy or wishes to be rushed.

The same person in a group, exhilarated by the presence of friends, can take a completely different personality. Instead of being impersonal with the server, he or she is now friendly.

If the group is large and made up of relative strangers, as in a banquet setting, the server may become a non-person, with customers referring to him or her in the third person even when the server is nearby and can overhear the comments. No one likes to be treated in such a manner, although one's background may condition the person for such treatment so that he/she finds it acceptable. Servers may set themselves up sometimes for such treatment by displaying a lack of self-confidence, excessive deference or overeagerness. Something in human nature, at least in some people, causes them to treat such people as inferiors and even to humiliate them.

One of the reasons visitors to this country are surprised by the service, especially in the West, is that the service person often genuinely feels equal to or better than the customer; certainly the service person's health may be superior. Many times the financial and educational level of the server is higher as well.

The Hard Sell

Restaurant literature and educational programs uniformly urge service personnel to promote and sell as part of the service job. The rationale is that sales and tips will increase. Discussions with servers bear out the thesis, but there are some qualifications. Undoubtedly, some customers have a fixed idea of how much they will spend on a particular meal, and such people may resent a hard sell, such as "Would you like a cocktail?" "Will you have dessert?" "Will you have an after-dinner liqueur?" Some people may feel pressured and sometimes say so, especially if the approach by the server is hard sell. Those who receive a higher check than expected may avoid the restaurant in the future.

The type of clientele may determine the best approach,

hard or soft sell. Low-key, complete service may be what is expected. Other patrons, wanting to "live it up," may welcome the hard sell and purposely run up the tab as a kind of self-indulgence. "Nothing is too good for our anniversary," "my business client" or "prospective buyer." The expense-account tab, using the company's money, is the excuse to have the best available.

Servers characteristically compete with each other in the amount of tips received in the course of a work shift. Some servers make 50 or even 100 percent more than others. Obviously, the service rendered has been perceived by the diner as superior, or the server has manipulated the diner into increasing the check or the tip percentage, or both. Tip and tab go together. Management mostly pushes the thought, "When in doubt, promote."

Aside from "selling," service includes a number of other factors and practices, including showmanship, ritualization of wine service, paying attention to what is said by the diner, attention to detail, refilling water glasses, cleaning ashtrays, replacing soiled silver and so on. The server is attempting to control the behavior of the diner. Call it manipulation, influencing attitude, making friends, maintaining rapport or what have you; it is still "selling."

A server who displays skill and confidence is obviously desirable. In most situations, a harassed or timid server may elicit sympathy, but may also arouse apprehension or uneasiness in the customer. No doubt, a number of customers want to be courted and wooed, buttered up and even fawned upon. Others may resent this obvious kind of behavior.

A research study of the ability of servers to influence diner behavior compared a control group which was not subject to the "promote and sell treatment" with a group which was given the hard-sell treatment. High-priced items were recommended to the latter group: specifics concerning cocktails, appetizers and main courses were suggested. Desserts or after-dinner drinks were promoted.

The control group of diners was treated to a "non-manipulative" type of service. When any of the members of the dining party asked "What's good?" they were politely reminded that everything was good. Two phrases used extensively for this group were, "Are you ready to order?" and "Would anyone care for anything else?" The server was as attentive and available as for the experimental group; however, the server's behavior was marked by lack of initiative. Diner groups were divided into three broad age categories; young (20-34), middle-age (35-55) or older (55 or older). The older diner had been stereotyped as a poor promotional prospect as compared with the younger group. The study took place at a leisure dining restaurant with a high-check average in a summer resort in the Northeast United States.

The results of the study showed that, indeed, young parties did spend and tip more than the older group. Middle-aged foursomes ran up the highest tab, middle-aged pairs the lowest. The experimental group, the ones subjected to manipulative control, had significantly higher tabs. The expected happened: the "promoting server not only maximizes his/her returns, but more important he/she is able to exercise a measure of control over the reward structure governing his/her work."

Formal or Informal?

How formal should the relations between host or hostess and guest be? Should the server be seen and not heard? Does the customer want formality or informality?

The answers vary.

Some restaurants thrive on informality. The servers may appear in tennis shoes and blue jeans saying, "Hi, I'm Bob, I'll be your waiter tonight. Please call upon me for anything I can do to make your meal pleasant."

In another, more formal atmosphere, the waiter may speak only when spoken to. His conversation may be limited to, "Good evening, Madam; good evening, Sir." "I hope you enjoy your meal, Madam," etc.

Some general principles apply to all restaurants:

Restaurants, by their nature, are service oriented, and all personnel should accept this as a continuing challenge to give excellent service.

Complaints should be accepted at face value, at least until proven to be without substance.

The viewpoint of the customer is different from that of the employee or the manager. Most complaints are left unspoken. When a complaint is voiced, it could be a public relations opportunity. Unsatisfactory food should be replaced at once with another of the same or of the customer's choice. A complimentary bottle of wine or an after-dinner liqueur adds a gracious note.

Never try to explain why things go wrong. A customer is not interested in excuses.

A famous maitre d', Oscar of the Waldorf, considered himself a stage manager. He would often approach a table, examine the food and, even if nothing was wrong, would add some little touch or would have it whisked away and replaced. Servers were trained to focus on him. Hand signals let the servers know what to do. His mien was grave concern for the customer's well-being. He was very polite, very formal, very "tuned in" to the guest.

CONCLUSION TO PART I

The next two decades will be witness to many significant changes in the hospitality and service industries. Primarily there will be tremendous growth in facilities involved in the services. This will cause great increases in the demand for persons to staff the many jobs and positions that will come available in this expanding work arena. However, the numbers of people entering the service field will decrease significantly. Not only will demand for a shrinking labor force go up, but also many service operations will fail for lack of recognition of the need for training in one major area; human relations, defined in this book as the combination of guest and employee relations.

In PART I, emphasis has been placed on acquainting the reader with the hospitality industry, (a major part of the service industry), and all of the various elements of guest relations that might be experienced in the hospitality world of hotels, restaurants and related endeavors. The general subject of "courtesy" was investigated, along with many possible experiences in communicating with members of the service staff found in the "front of the house" (a term commonly used when identifying hotel staff members who work in prime guest contact areas). Special industry problem areas are exposed and treated with the expertise and skilled experience of many veterans. But in most cases, common sense, caring and the Golden Rule win out as a proper guide for actions relating to other human beings.

In the 1970's and 1980's there was an explosion in the number of colleges and universities offering conceptual presentations (and degrees) in Hotel, Restaurant and Service Administration. Technical competence in the various ground-roots aspects of service (such as concern for the guest) has, however, been left to the many hotel companies who hire these school graduates. It is quite possible, however, that the decade of the nineties will see a growth in the United States of institutions specializing in the formal service and human relations training of persons involved in the service industries; much as can be found in the great hotel schools of Europe. In the meantime, it will do well for service companies to remember the value of that Golden Rule and think "the people business" along with "profits."

To ensure that the reader absorbs the many examples of guest services encountered in PART I, it is suggested that the questions posed in APPENDIX B be reviewed. In every question, it is suggested that the reader place him or herself in the position of a "front of the house" service employee as they go about answering the questions. If difficulty is encountered, they should then place themselves in the position of the guest, and think, Golden Rule. Answers to the questions in the APPENDIX will then become much more obvious.

ENDNOTES

1. Athey, Thomas H. et al., *Structured Systems Approach*, 1980.

PART II

TRANSACTIONAL ANALYSIS
AN ANALYTICAL TOOL FOR GUEST RELATIONS

INTRODUCTION

In Part I, we looked at guest relations from a practical and common-sense viewpoint. In this section, we will discuss Transactional Analysis[1] or TA, as it is called in the business and professional world, as a way of looking at all face-to-face and some written communications. According to Muriel James and associates,[2] TA can provide us with a method of analyzing personal communications (Transactions) between people, and creates for us a tool or system of analysis that can be applied equally to both guest and employee relations in the hospitality industry.

As a tool or frame of reference, TA can help us expedite and smooth out guest relations. It can help us avoid misunderstanding, defuse potentially explosive situations and help guests feel better about themselves and the hospitality industry with which they are doing business. Being able to properly analyze transactions and apply learned TA techniques then becomes the basis for success in accomplishing desired end results as we communicate. TA can promote better understanding, help set and achieve realistic goals, cause us to initiate rational thinking when necessary, and move forward in logical fashion when engaged in problem solving activities.

TA can be thought of as a means of developing tact, and tactful people have been sensitive to other people's feelings since time immemorial. They listen carefully and respond thoughtfully to what is said by the other person in face-to-face communications. Tactful people are aware of their own feelings at the moment of communications, or, in terms of TA, "where they themselves are coming from." They also are aware of the other person's feelings, or "where that person is coming from." In TA terms, they are aware of their own and the other person's "ego state." An ego state might best be described as a momentary or habitual "mental set" that is in existence within the person at the time a given communication takes place, affecting thought processes, attitudes, behavior and performance.

TA can sharpen our perceptions of these ego states by providing a model to follow, a model carried around in the head, a handy-dandy guide to guest and employee relations. The brighter and more perceptive the user, the more effective the use of the model.

TA's Relation to Psychoanalysis and Psychology

TA draws upon psychology and psychoanalysis and is widely taught, even though its formal theory was not put together until the 1950s by Eric Berne.[3] Its detailed development does not concern us. Suffice it to say that modern psychoanalysis was conceived around the turn of the century on Sigmund Freud's couch. Freud, a Viennese psychiatrist, and later his students, studied maladjusted people and pointed out that much of our behavior is influenced by past emotional experiences, many of which we may not be aware of. The personality, Freud said, can be thought of as having three parts: the Id, the Ego and the Superego - a model, if you will, of the mind or psyche.

Berne also developed a three-part model, or construct; the PARENT, the ADULT and the CHILD, or PAC model. Freud's model - Id, Ego and Superego - suggested the TA model PAC. The Id, Freud said, is the source of unstructured emotion - our animal instincts and propensities. It has elements of TA's CHILD. Freud's Superego or conscience suggests the CRITICAL PARENT in the PAC model. Berne, however, isolated and defined the basic "unit" by which the psychotherapeutic sciences are today thought to be more "scientific." The unit of measurement as defined by Berne was "A unit of social inter-course known as a Transaction." For example - if two or more people encounter each other, sooner or later one of them will speak or give some indication of acknowledging the presence of the other(s). This is called a TRANSACTION STIMULUS. Another person will then say or do something which is in some way related to the stimulus. This is called a TRANSAC-TION RESPONSE. TRANSACTIONAL ANALYSIS is, then, a method of examining the one situation wherein "I do or say something to you," and "you do or say something back," at the same time *determining which part of the multiple natured individual or personality is "coming on."* To give the PAC model a Walt Disney flavor, the PARENT, ADULT and CHILD can be thought of as three little people carried around in our heads who influence and often direct our behavior. Muriel James and associates indicated that our ego states are states of being; not roles but psychological realities.

TA is also a method of systematizing the information derived from analyzing these transactions in words which have the same meaning for everyone who is using them. Agreement on the meaning of words, plus agreement of what to examine, are the two keys which have unlocked the doors to the "mysteries of why people do as they do."

In his early work, Berne observed that as you watch and listen to people, you can see them change before your eyes. The child who can't make the toy work, the girl who waits for the phone call, the man who turns pale when hearing that his business is failing. All such events can bring out a different ego state as events unfold in our lives at a given time.

ENDNOTES

1. Eric Berne, *Transactional Analysis in Psychotherapy: A System-atic Individual and Social Psychiatry;* (New York: Grove Press, 1961).

2. Muriel James, et al., *Techniques in Transactional Analysis For Psychotherapists and Counselors;* (Reading, MASS: Addison-Wesley, 1971), Muriel James and Dorothy Jongeward, *Born To Win: Transactional Analysis with Gestalt Experiments,* (Reading, MA Addison-Wesley, 1971) and Muriel James and Dorothy Jongeward, *The People Book; Transactional Analysis for Students* (Reading, MASS: Addison-Wesley, 1975).

3. Eric Berne, *ibid.* See also Eric Berne, *Games People Play: The Psychology of Human Relationships,* (New York: Grove Press, 1964).

CHAPTER 6

EGO STATES, TRANSACTIONS AND THE P A C MODEL[1]

The PARENT EGO (Critical and Nurturing)

The first ego state in TA terms is the PARENT. This ego state may be divided into two distinct subdivisions known as the CRITICAL Parent or the NURTURING Parent; sometimes thought of, respectively, as the "bossy" or the "mothering" side of the personality.

The PARENT is a huge collection of "recordings" in the brain of unquestioned or imposed external events perceived by a person in early years (from birth through adolescence). Everything the young person sees his or her parents (or persons in authority) do, and everything they are heard to say, is recorded in the PARENT ego. Everyone has a PARENT since no one can grow in a life vacuum; all have experienced external stimuli.

The PARENT is specific in every person. It is that tape of data based on individual early experiences that is taken in and recorded straightway without editing. Mother-Father become internalized in our PARENT as tapes of our childhood experiences are created. Taped is what the parent said or did, as well as our having lived through certain situation dynamics. In the PARENT are recorded all of the admonitions, rules and laws that the child hears from the parents, and the perceived observations of the parents' behavior.

Also recorded are all of the other forms of communication, from tone of voice, facial expressions, cuddling or non-cuddling, to the more elaborate verbal rules and regulations espoused by those in authority. As the infant begins to understand language, thousands of "no's" and repeated "don'ts" create a bombardment, only to give way to looks of pain and horror in mother's face when clumsiness brings shame on the family in the form of aunt Ethel's broken antique vase. Likewise are recorded the coos of pleasure of a happy mother and the looks of delight of a proud father (the nurturing side of the PARENT).

As we grow and mature, we are instructed in what is acceptable behavior - right and wrong, good and bad. Now come the more complicated pronouncements, such as "Remember son, wherever you go in life, you will always find that the best people are Methodists. Never tell a lie. Pay your bills. You're a good girl if you clean your plate. Never trust a woman. Do unto others, as or before they do unto you." Also within the parent is the "inconsistency of hypocrisy." The parent may say "don't smoke" while smoking or proclaim a religious ethic but not act accordingly. Since it is not safe to question this inconsistency, children defend their sanity by "turning off the recording."

These instructions then become our moral code and are incorporated into the mind as the conscience, or, in Freudian terms, the SUPEREGO. Some people cannot accept behavior contrary to what they have been taught, and they react to this behavior as a CRITICAL PARENT. In TA, this is the CRITICAL PARENT:

"Sit up straight."

"You're doing that wrong."

"Drink your milk and don't spill."

"Put on your rubbers."

"Keep quiet, I'm talking."

"That's stupid."

"You shouldn't."

"Believe me, I know what's best for you."

"In my judgment you should . . ."

"All salespeople are crooks."

All cliches fit the mold of the CRITICAL PARENT. They require no original thought; just an open mouth and a propensity to repeat what others have said many times before.

Humankind undoubtedly has an instinctive nurturing part in its personality. This is the NURTURING PARENT.

"You look tired. I'll finish cleaning your room."

"Let me help you."

"Don't cry, everything will be all right."

"I'll do it for you."

"Poor baby."

Most societies encourage the need to nurture and to help those who appear to need help.[2]

The CHILD EGO (Adaptive, Free or Natural and Rebel)

We come into the world with a bundle of instincts and propensities which are later curbed, channeled or repressed to a greater or lesser degree by civilization. Freud called these instincts the Id. In TA, the CHILD ego is at the seat of our feelings and emotions.

While external events are being recorded straightway and unedited into the PARENT tape, there is another recording being made at the same instant. This is a tape of "internal events" which are representative of our attitudes, feelings, moods and emotions resulting directly our from having experienced the external stimuli. This tape is the internalized human response to what is seen, heard, experienced and felt, and it is identified as our CHILD Ego.

Since an infant has no vocabulary during the earliest of experiences, most reactions are in the form of feelings. Dependent, inept, clumsy and with no words with which to construct meanings or display understanding (or lack of it); the result is most times crying or cooing. Feelings of wetness or hunger usually bring the only form of expression available to an infant, crying. Comfort and enjoyment can only be expressed by cooing, or an instinctive smile.

As the infant grows, the bombardment of stimuli continues. Feelings represented in the CHILD begin to create more exact forms of expression known as emotions. A threefold division of these emotions begins to develop, in which case our inability to change or overcome dominating stimuli causes responses that say, "adapt or perish;" hence, the ADAPTIVE CHILD is displayed. Other feelings - joy, happiness, "the world is my oyster," "who cares?" or the elation of excitement - are identified as the FREE or NATURAL CHILD. Finally there is the angry, temper tantrum, rebellious type of response, labeled the REBEL CHILD.

Feelings are natural and need to be expressed. The repression of feelings can cause serious psychological problems that are better dealt with by the clinical psychologist or psychiatrist. The expression of feelings can be guided and controlled under most conditions, however, when recognized and properly identified. Whereas people coming from their CRITICAL PARENT may be reacting to behavior contrary to what they have been taught, the ADAPTIVE CHILD reacts out of feelings. This behavior would best be characterized by indications of timidity, shyness, uncertainty and a lack of self-confidence. People who give up easily or despair readily are adapting to the pressures perceived. Individuals inclined to "roll with the punches," unable to express themselves clearly, or who run words together, sometimes speaking in incomplete sentences are, in most cases, "coming from their ADAPTIVE CHILD."

In TA, this is the ADAPTIVE CHILD:

"I can't do anything right."

"I'm so confused. Will you help me?"

"I never seem to get ahead."

"Look after me."

"If only I could get that job, all my problems would be over."

"Everything happens to me."

Different feelings and emotions are expressed by someone in their FREE or NATURAL CHILD:

"Like me as I am."

"It's too nice a day to work. Let's knock off early."

"Hey, that's fantastic!"

"Who cares? It's quitting time."

And the REBEL CHILD:

"Give it to me now!"

"Listen, don't get smart with me."

"I hate you!"

"I won't do it!" (when said in anger).

The ADULT EGO

The third ego state in TA is the thinking, rational person called the ADULT. The ADULT is nonemotional, objective and problem-solving. When people "come from" their ADULT, they expect problems and solve them by using their intelligence, and without getting emotional. The only similarity between the ADULT and the PARENT and CHILD is that the ADULT, like the others, also had its beginnings early in our infant development.

At about ten months of age, a remarkable thing began to happen to us. We started to experience the power of locomotion and to manipulate objects. We freed ourselves from the prison of immobility. We moved out into our world to discover for ourselves what was there. This curiosity, experimentation and questioning was the beginning of the formation of the ADULT. Adult data are accumulated as the result of our ability to *find out for ourselves* what is "different" about life from what is "taught" (PARENT) and what is "felt" (CHILD).

The ADULT, then, is our thinking and reasoning state. We ask probing questions and listen for factual answers. Typical of the questioning would be the type that asks who, what, when, where, why and how. When in the ADULT, a person is relaxed, using good eye contact and is emotionless (conversation can be almost dull). When "giving" factual information, or in the act of making decisions, taking action and problem solving, we accomplish the task at hand while firmly in our ADULT.

An example, the washing machine stops washing. The homemaker inspects the machine and sees no solution. She phones the company from which the machine was purchased and asks that a service person come out. The service person inspects the machine and says the transmission "is out" and the cost of repairing the eight-year-old machine would be about $200. The ADULT decides it would be to her advantage to buy a new machine. She phones various appliance dealers and, after comparing price and quality, makes her choice. (Decision made.)

Take this problem situation: An automobile has a flat tire.

The CHILD despairs, "Oh, what luck! What am I going to do? Someone help me." (There may be tears or curses.)

The CRITICAL PARENT immediately thinks of someone to blame: "That tire company ought to be run out of business."

The ADULT thinks: "I can walk to a phone and call for help, or I can change the tire myself."

At any given time, a person can be described as coming

from one of these three ego states: the CHILD, the PARENT or the ADULT.

In guest relations, awareness of our own ego state and that of the guest gives us a leg up on the situation. No one can be sure about the other person's current ego state. Perhaps we are not even sure of our own ego state at a given moment. Even so, sensitivity to ego states and the consequences of the transaction underway can help improve the transactions that follow, and help to avoid unfruitful transactions and potentially dangerous ones.

Study the table that follows, then practice identifying ego states by doing Exercise 1.

ASPECTS OF EGO STATES

	CRITICAL PARENT	ADULT	CHILD
VOICE TONES	Talks down Critical Accusing Speaks with certainty	Matter of fact Objective Deliberate	Excited Overcome Quivering Interrupted
WORDS USED	You should You shouldn't Don't do Do this It's best that	How, What, When, Where, Why, Who It seems that This may be Probably	Great Terrible Help me I can't
POSTURES	Proper Erect Stiff	Attentive Reactive Alert	Slouched Humped-over Springy Bouncy
FACIAL EXPRESSIONS	Stern Inflexible Grave Determined	Alert, focused on the speaker	Excited Misty eyes Pouting mouth
BODY GESTURES	Hands on hips Pointed finger Arms folded across chest Emphatic	Leans forward to the other person to hear and see better Needs to indicate understanding	Hands active Jumping Laughing Crying

EXERCISE 1

IDENTIFYING EGO STATES

IN THIS EXERCISE, YOU WILL SEE 16 BRIEF ILLUSTRATIONS OF THE VARIOUS EGO STATES. CIRCLE THE LETTER TO THE LEFT OF EACH STATEMENT WHICH IDENTIFIES THE EGO STATE YOU THINK THE SPEAKER IS USING.

P A C Well, he may be a nice guy, but I wouldn't want to turn my back on him.

P A C Boy, you're never going to believe what I just found out!

P A C I don't think I can make a decision until I've considered all the alternatives.

P A C I've just gotta go. Everything depends on it.

P A C Woman driver, huh? It figures.

P A C I've checked your report thoroughly, and I think you've done a fine job.

P A C Believe me, I know what's best for you.

P A C Oh, if only I could get that promotion and bonus, all my problems would be solved.

P A C If you can't do something right, don't bother doing it at all.

P   A   C   You think you feel bad - just listen to what happened to me.

P   A   C   I really don't know what to do. Can you give me some more information?

P   A   C   Come on, why don't you let me do that for you?

P   A   C   The party really would be fun, but I've made a commitment to finish this job. I think I'll stay and get it out of the way.

P   A   C   Hey, that's fantastic. Wish I'd thought of that.

P   A   C   I know you're upset about the new schedule, but don't worry about it. Things will get better.

P   A   C   Don't blame me; I don't make the rules around here.

THE P A C MODEL

Having first identified the attributes of the PARENT, CHILD and ADULT, a framework is now necessary in which TA can be put to work. This is done by first accepting the fact that, to one degree or another, all human beings have within themselves all of the ego states described, along with each of their variations. None of us escape what might appear to be "bad," nor are we blessed with only that which appears to be all "good." While it is true that some people "live" in certain ego states more than they do others, each of us has a little of everything, or a little bit of every place "to come from." Because there will be times when we initiate transactions, and times when we will respond, there must be a system whereby we can identify a given role in TA. This is done with the PAC model. Graphically the PARENT, ADULT, CHILD model called PAC is seen as:

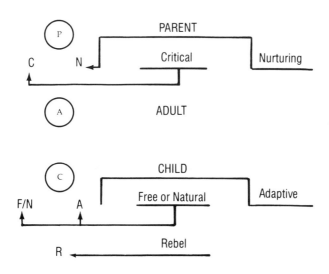

When two people are engaged in a transaction, one is the sender, the other the receiver. Any face-to-face communication is called a transaction.

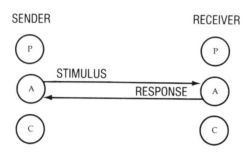

Note that the respondent becomes equally endowed with the PAC.

Aiming Transactions

Consider the sender and receiver of communications: when the sender originates a transaction stimulus, it is done from a specific ego state. It is also "aimed" at a specific ego state in the receiver. When the receiver communicates, the transaction response is also aimed from a specific ego state in the receiver back to a specific ego state in the sender of the initial communication.

COMPLEMENTARY TRANSACTIONS

When the response to a transaction stimulus comes from the ego state at which it was aimed, and is directed back to the ego state in the sender where it was originated, the communication is said to be a COMPLEMENTARY TRANSACTION. In COMPLEMENTARY transactions, it is said that both sender and receiver get the results desired and, as a result, communications *will stay open*. Additionally, when COMPLEMENTARY transactions occur in ADULT to ADULT communications, objective action can take place, decisions can be made, choices

established and problems solved. Even when no problem resolution takes place in CHILD to CHILD, PARENT to PARENT or
PARENT to CHILD transactions, they may nevertheless be
COMPLEMENTARY and, as a result, communications *will*
remain open.

Let's diagram a simple COMPLEMENTARY TRANSAC-
TION:

A customer approaches a hostess in a restaurant. The
hostess originates the first transaction as the sender and says,
"Good evening, sir. Welcome to the Jolly Pig." (The guest
expects the hostess to initiate the transaction and to direct the
seating, since the hostess is the expert providing service.)

This is a reasonable, non-manipulative message, more an
opener or ritual expressing friendliness. In TA terms, the
hostess is coming from the ADULT ego state. The hostess
expects the guest to respond in kind by saying, "Hello,"
"Good evening" or something similar. The hostess expects the
guest to also "come from" the ADULT ego state. If the guest
responds as expected, the transaction is COMPLEMENTARY
and can be diagrammed:

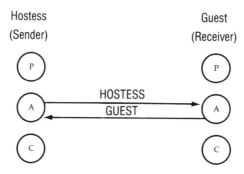

CROSSED TRANSACTIONS

Suppose, however, the guest is feeling hostile toward things in general and responds, "What's good about it?" The guest is not coming from the ADULT ego as expected, but either from the CRITICAL PARENT ego state (example 1 below), or perhaps from the complaining, helpless CHILD ego state (example 2). The transaction has been "crossed," and would be diagrammed as follows:

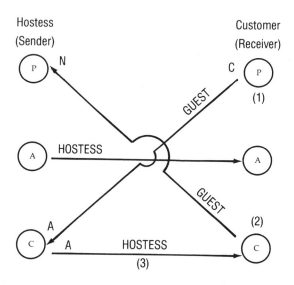

Such a response can be unnerving and taken as a personal affront. The hostess becomes upset and says, "Well, I was only trying to be friendly" (example 3). The hostess may have responded by coming from the CHILD, and subsequent transactions could be "HOOKED" into CHILD to CHILD or PARENT to CHILD communications.

CROSSED TRANSACTIONS, then, are those transactions in which the sender *does not* get the desired results. In most cases, when this happens communications either break down or get hopelessly HOOKED into PARENT to CHILD or CHILD to CHILD relations.

Crossing to the ADULT

Applying the TA model, the transaction becomes a challenge for the hostess. How can the hostess move the guest back to the ADULT ego state, uncrossing the transactions?

The hostess can ignore the CHILD response and, provided there is time, smile and continue:

"I hope you had a pleasant drive here," or

"Would you like a table by the window?"

Any question which objectively seeks or gives information, has no hidden motive and is reasonable tends to activate the thinking part of the mind, the ADULT. Crossing to the ADULT, then, is the exception whereby communication does not break down, but creates a new opportunity for objectivity and rational thinking to resume.

Review of COMPLEMENTARY and CROSSED TRANSACTIONS

When transactions are COMPLEMENTARY:

1. Both sender and recipient gain the desired results of communicating, and communications will stay open.

2. Although communications may be COMPLEMENTARY in CHILD to CHILD, PARENT to PARENT or PARENT to CHILD, and may continue, nothing of an objective nature will be accomplished.

3. If communications are COMPLEMENTARY in ADULT to ADULT conversations, action can ensue, conclusions can be reached and problems can be solved.

When transactions are CROSSED:

1. Either sender or receiver, or both, do not get the results desired from communicating, and communications either break down, or become hopelessly "HOOKED" into CHILD to CHILD or PARENT to CHILD relations.

2. If transactions are CROSSED to the ADULT, communications not only will remain open, but will also provide a new framework in which relations can be improved, decisions can be reached and action can be taken where necessary.

THE ULTERIOR TRANSACTION

There is a third and sometimes more difficult type of transaction to identify, known as the ULTERIOR TRANSACTION. This type of transaction may be hidden within either the COMPLEMENTARY or CROSSED transaction, and is used by either the sender or receiver when intent on playing a "psychological game" of some sort. The ULTERIOR TRANSACTION heralds the "hidden motive" whereby subtleness may be used to gain a "payoff" in the form of having either one's CHILD or PARENT ego state "stroked."

The ULTERIOR TRANSACTION may eventually become recognizable as a delayed type of put-down, criticism or insensitivity to the needs of the other person.

To say one thing while intent on meaning something quite different is to be adept in producing the ULTERIOR TRANSACTION; a characteristic not conducive to meaningful communications in either the personal or professional world.

Consider the example of the front desk clerk who must tell the guest, "I'm sorry, sir, but due to expected departures that did not materialize, we will be unable to honor your guaranteed reservation. We will, however, be able to put you up in the hotel across the street, which is quite nice, and the service is comparable to ours."

The guest responds by saying:

"Thank you, but I don't know where there could ever be a hotel with service comparable to yours."

Is the guest being genuine in his comment (ADULT response to the ADULT efforts of the desk clerk to resolve a problem)? Or, is the guest being sarcastic and coming from the CRITICAL PARENT ego state in hopes of making the desk clerk feel small and insecure?

For practice in aiming transactions, do Exercise 2 at this time:

EXERCISE 2

DIAGRAMMING TRANSACTIONS

IN EACH OF THE FOLLOWING TRANSACTIONS, INDI-CATE BY USE OF AN ARROW WHERE THE FIRST COMMUNICATION ORIGINATES AND WHERE IT IS AIMED. DO THE SAME FOR THE SECOND COMMUNICA-TION.

TRANSACTION 1: (Example)

1. I just got this month's capital expense report and I just can't figure out any of the statistics.
2. Don't ask me for help. I'm still trying to decipher my own figures.

P P
A A
C C

TRANSACTION 2:

1. You look exhausted. Why don't you take a break?
2. Thanks, but I'm so swamped, I just don't think I can take the time.

P P
A A
C C

TRANSACTION 3:

1. If you expect to get anywhere around here, your work is going to have to improve.
2. Can you give me any suggestions about what I can do to improve my performance?

P P
A A
C C

TRANSACTION 4:

1. Just like always. The meeting started 20 minutes late.
2. As if we didn't have anything better to do.

P P
A A
C C

TRANSACTION 5:

1. How do you expect me to transfer your calls if you don't let me know where you are?

2. If you'd check your messages once in a while, you'd find out I was in Mr. Black's office.

P P
A A
C C

TRANSACTION 6:

1. Do you know where the Jasper file is?

2. Right on your desk. Honestly, I don't know how you'd find anything without me.

P P
A A
C C

TRANSACTION 7:

1. What do you think of the new promotional campaign?

2. I'm not sure yet. I really haven't studied it well enough to understand it thoroughly.

P P
A A
C C

TRANSACTION 8:

1. I can't believe it — the department is already ahead of quota for the month.

2. No kidding? Hey, does that mean we can knock off early today?

P P
A A
C C

TRANSACTION 9:

1. We do need a manager for that new project, but you may not be ready for it.

2. I'm sure I can handle it.

P P
A A
C C

TRANSACTION 10:

1. I don't know what I'm going to do. The report is due at 3 PM today, and I'm not going to make it.

2. I've got some free time. Why don't I give you a hand?

P P
A A
C C

TRANSACTION 11:

1. Do you think we'll have time to review the new budget this afternoon?

2. Boy, I hope not. It's gorgeous outside, and I don't feel like working.

P P
A A
C C

TRANSACTION 12:

1. Poor Tom. They did it to him again. Passed him up for another promotion.

2. But I understand the man they promoted is really well-qualified.

P P
A A
C C

Where is the Person Coming From?

Having now been exposed to the various types of ego states and types of transactions, is the model complete? Do simple "words" give all the clues needed to determine which part of the multi-natured personality is in operation? How can we tell for sure which EGO STATE a person is coming from? The words spoken are the best indicator, but the way they are spoken, the inflections used, the accompanying gestures and the posture of the speaker may provide the real clues to the ego state.

The simple word "Hello" can come from PARENT, ADULT or CHILD. It can be an ordinary word of greeting as a salutation coming from the ADULT. It can be sarcastic and critical, coming from the CRITICAL PARENT. Or it can be exuberant and bouncy, expressing the unfettered and happy CHILD. Inflection and tone of voice override words. Body language, as previously mentioned, speaks truer than words.

In using TA, the employee is constantly being asked two questions: "Where am I coming from?" and "Where is the guest coming from?"

Two observers of the same transactions may come up with different conclusions. The simple question, "If you're not too busy, will you help me?", could be coming from the CHILD or it could be coming from the ADULT, depending upon the situation and the way the sentence is expressed. How the sender acts at the time and the voice inflection offer clues as to the ego state involved. Also there is a possibility that the person is merely acting, and that "real feelings" are being carefully cloaked.

Identifying the CHILD depends to a large extent on determining whether or not emotions are being expressed, for the CHILD carries an emotional load; feelings that can be sensed by the other person. Additionally, when CHILD feelings are being aroused or heightened in an individual, it is more than likely someone's PARENT ego that is causing it. Of course, old poker face may be boiling mad inside and the giddy girl may be perfectly calm and calculating.

There is also the matter of cultural control placed on the expression of emotions. People from different societies express themselves differently. Italians, for example, are known for their hand and face gestures while speaking. In the U.S., it is not good form for men to cry or faint in public; women may do so. Other societies train the individual to hide all emotional display. The careful observer catches small clues that help to place the person in a particular ego state.

The Power of the Tone of Voice

Here is another example of the importance of analyzing the tone of voice. A librarian spots a patron tearing sections out of a newspaper and approaches the person with "May I help you?"

The "May I help you?" can be said accusingly and be well understood by the library patron as being admonition rather than inquiry. The librarian is coming from the CRITICAL PARENT talking to the CHILD.

An attractive female customer parades into a department store in shorts. The bright-eyed male employee says, "May I help you?" The tone of voice could well imply CHILD to

CHILD and be more invitation than question.

Regardless of tone of voice and good intentions, whatever is said can be misinterpreted by the receiver. The motive involved at the moment in any given transaction is often difficult - if not impossible - to ascertain by the receiver. In other words, "Meanings are in people, they are not in words."

TA puts a label on an ego state - PARENT, ADULT, CHILD - but cannot identify for certain the motive behind the transaction. In some circumstances, identification of motive may be impossible without knowing the person and the situation extremely well. A customer may appear disdainful, but the disdain could be based on insecurity. Aggression and hostility can be based on insecurity. Aggression and hostility can be based on fear, as well as anger or resentment.

The same caveat holds true for crossed transactions. That they are crossed, that the receiver sends back an unexpected message or changes from one ego state to another, may be a fact. The reason for that crossing may not be apparent at all. TA can help spot crossed transactions, but cannot necessarily indicate why they are crossed.

As fatigue increases on the job, it is more difficult to come from the ADULT. The temptation is to switch from ADULT to PARENT or CHILD. This is quite natural. The CHILD is the part of us which acts on impulse, which responds in anger or in joy, quickly and without reference to the ADULT. The PARENT is also ready and eager to appear. The PARENT is the moralizing person, the programmed person with the catalog of taboos, rules and regulations that have been incorporated over a lifetime. Under stress, it is easier to judge than to try to hook the other person's ADULT. It may also be easier to join the other person's CHILD, fretting, disparaging, sulking or removing oneself from responsibility. It is the CHILD who thinks someone else is responsible: "They" have caused all the trouble. The CHILD is the "helpless me." Under pressure, the CHILD may throw a tantrum, whine, cry or even physically attack.

EXERCISE 2 might be reviewed at this time to determine other interpretations that might be placed on several of the transactions if voice tones or inflections are taken into consideration.

The PARENT Can Be Appropriate on Occasion

There is one occasion when PARENT to PARENT complementary transactions might be appropriate. Normally, such communications herald one of those "psychological games" that people sometimes play called "Ain't it Awful" (more will be said later about "games"). To play "Ain't it Awful," both the sender and receiver must select a third person, thing or event to criticize. "Ain't it Awful" is the only kind of "game" that may be played in which neither the sender nor receiver will be harmed. It is not recommended that service personnel engage in playing this game when a third person is to be criticized. When the guest is criticizing a thing happening or an event, however, the service person acknowledging the same past personal feeling sometimes tends to relax the guest or soften the moment. For example: Consider the hotel driver or bellperson who goes to the airport to pick up a guest. The employee opens the conversation by saying:

"Good afternoon, Mr. Jones. May I take your bags?" (ADULT ritual statement, ADULT question asked.)

Mr. Jones replies, "Good afternoon; thank you." (hands bags to employee) (ADULT ritual statement, ADULT reply.)

The employee then says, "How was your flight from New York?" (ADULT question.)

Mr. Jones: "That was one of the worst flights I have ever had. The weather was horrible, service lousy on the flight and they lost my luggage when I transferred in New York." (PARENT criticism of the weather, flight service and airport luggage handling, aimed at the PARENT ego in the employee.)

The employee, sensing a need for agreement, responds, "I know how you feel. That weather can be treacherous at times. I

141

had a bad experience myself once due to the weather. Will you be staying with us for a few days?" (PARENT to PARENT agreement, judging the weather, playing "Ain't it Awful" with the guest. The employee not wanting to criticize the airline service or the airport in New York, then gently changes the subject by asking another ADULT question.)

Although PARENT to PARENT transactions at times have their merit, employees must be careful when engaging the guest in such a manner. Such comments are best limited to a simple, "I know how you feel," making sure that the response is "nurturing" and not "critical."

The CHILD Can Also Be Appropriate

Obviously, life would be pretty dull if all transactions were on the ADULT to ADULT level. Certainly all CRITICAL PARENT transactions would make for a grim world. Enthusiasm, laughter and joy are part of the CHILD. How many auto sales would be made if the salesman did not at least partially come from the CHILD? Parties would be a big drag without a lot of children around. Alcohol releases the CHILD, but not knowing "which CHILD" makes alcohol a dubious method for improving the party.

In a business situation, however, the CHILD must be handled with care.

According to the real estate agent, "This is the best house in the neighborhood."

"You're going to love the pecan pie," says the bakery clerk.

"This restaurant serves the greatest clam chowder in the East."

The car salesperson: "You've got the greatest buy in the world!"

These statements are probably exaggeration - and may come from the CHILD. Yet they express enthusiasm, warmth and good will - and can be entirely appropriate.

Ordinarily, a reasonable question will be referred to the guest's ADULT for processing. Questions are often effective in shifting ego states to the ADULT; but not always. The question may come from the CHILD. If it does, it is usually a question begging patronization. The question can also be part of an ULTERIOR TRANSACTION - one that says one thing but means something else. Suppose the employee says:

"Do you have a credit card?"

The guest's reply could be loaded with suspicion: "Why do you ask that?"

People often express hostility with sarcasm or raise all sorts of innuendoes with questions.

The innocent question may be anything but innocent, and may have the effect of raising an issue or calling attention to personal shortcomings or to somebody else's malpractice or misdeeds. Nevertheless, asking questions can refocus a conversation, moving it from an inappropriate ego state to one appropriate for the situation.

Hooking the ADULT

A question should be sincere, reasonable and pointed at getting the transaction back to or keeping the transaction on the ADULT level.

When transactions are seen as getting nowhere or hooking the CHILD to CHILD, or PARENT, change the subject:

Guest: "The last time I came here was one of the worst experiences I have had."

Desk Clerk: "I'm sure that won't happen again. I see you're from Chicago. Did you have a nice trip?"

Improving Transactions (the ADULT as Monitor)

Service personnel can use their ADULT to monitor transactions taking place, making sure to come from the ADULT. When the guest comes from the CHILD or PARENT, the employee notices the fact and can change the conversation so as to redirect transactions to the ADULT level, if indeed that is what is called for. Adult questions or statements help both the service employee and the guest "hit the core" of a problem. Such action always starts the thinking process. It is important, however, to be firmly in one's ADULT ego and not let the PARENT or CHILD get hooked.

To repeat, all business transactions need not be from the ADULT. Much of the fun in life comes from the CHILD, and none of us can avoid being the CRITICAL PARENT from time to time. The purpose of TA is to get the business of business accomplished and, in doing so, make the experience the most enjoyable possible for all concerned.

Even when coming from the PARENT or the CHILD, that part of the brain known as the frontal lobes, probably the home of the ADULT, is usually there. (It had better be.) The ADULT, the rational part of the mind, should be a disembodied over-seer of all transactions, saying, "Hold on now, use your head, think it out, don't get carried away." Under extreme emotion, the ADULT is completely blacked out. It's "watch out" time. Anything can happen.

The NURTURING PARENT

Many guests are reaching out for a NURTURING PARENT in the person of the service employee who makes the guest feel wanted and, yes, loved. Because of socialization, and a stereotypical myth, women have in the past been thought to be more NURTURING than men but this has been proven false. In fact, men have become recognized by enlightened companies as equally NURTURING and do just as well in guest contact areas, provided their verbal skills and problem solving abilities are well-developed. Both men and women in the service industry enjoy the NURTURING PARENT role.

The author recalls an occasion when a young male guest created a major scene in the lobby of a hotel. Because of his highly emotional and aggressive state, however, it was difficult to determine exactly what the problem was. It appeared that the only thing seeming important to the young man was to continue to rave. A male desk clerk remembered the young guest from earlier in the day when he had been in the hotel to arrange for a room and bottle of champagne for his wedding night that night. As the young guest stopped to take a breath, the desk clerk quickly inserted, "I know exactly how you feel; my wedding night got all fouled up too." (A NURTURING PARENT statement.) Hearing this, the young guest stopped talking and in the pause, the desk clerk continued, "Sir, please step back here into my office and tell me exactly what has happened. I'll do everything I can to straighten out the problem." As the young guest moved into the office his rage subsided and with surprise, he asked, "Did they foul you up too by forgetting the champagne?" The desk clerk quickly asked, "Is that what has happened to you here tonight?" "Yes," replied the young guest. "I drove 150 miles to get here this morning to make these arrangements which was to include an iced bucket of champagne. Then I drove 150 miles back to get married. Then another 150 miles to get back here, as quickly as I could! And, when I get here, and there wasn't any champagne, the only obvious thing in the room was the bed. I was humiliated in front of my bride."

Again, the desk clerk exclaimed, "It seems inevitable that someone or something has to happen to foul things up on a man's wedding night. I certainly can understand your anger in this case, (Another NURTURING PARENT statement.) I think I know exactly how to solve this problem. I'll be at your door in ten minutes with the champagne, and it will be my pleasure to serve it personally." (ADULT decision.)

The writer also recalls another incident when a female front desk manager at a large Chicago airport property was to be promoted to front office manager. According to company policy, she would be transferred to a smaller company property upon acceptance of the promotion. The lady manager, to the dismay of the resident manager, refused the promotion.

When asked why, her reply was, "Because I'd miss the hassle." She further elaborated as to how much she enjoyed her job, because every day there would be several guest contact problems that she would have to unsnarl, and it was this need to solve people problems that intrigued her the most. She was afraid that a smaller property would not provide her with the same challenge. The young manager was encouraged to reconsider her decision, which she did, and was later reported to notice just as many challenges for NURTURING in the smaller properties as she had become accustomed to in Chicago.

A Review of TA Terminology

TRANSACTIONS (Stimuli and Responses):

Whenever one individual speaks to another, or the other person responds, a transaction has taken place. Transactions are on a verbal and visual level, including body language. What is said may be straightforward and easily understood, or may be convoluted and have several levels of meaning or purpose. Transactions have various purposes, such as giving and getting information, problem solving, expressing feelings, giving strokes and playing psychological games.

EGO STATES:

Transactions come from one of three EGO STATES: PARENT, ADULT or CHILD; and are aimed at similar EGO STATES in the receiver of a transaction.

The PARENT includes those behaviors learned from parent figures - mother, father, teachers, clergy, the moral codes of the society. The PARENT, though emotionless, is often opinionated and prejudiced. The PARENT knows what is right and what is wrong, what behavior is acceptable, what is not. The PARENT, incorporated into the mind, forms conscience.

There are two PARENTS: the CRITICAL PARENT and the NURTURING PARENT.

The CRITICAL PARENT uses words such as "should," "don't," and "if I were you."

The CRITICAL PARENT is stern, uncompromising, the voice of morality and authority.

The NURTURING PARENT expresses sympathy, fatherly or motherly advice, "I'll take care of you," "Let me help you," "I sympathize with you."

The CHILD is the feeling and emotional part of us, usually spontaneous; it is the child in us who wants to play, have fun, be irresponsible. The child is quick to sulk, brood, pout or shout.

The ADULT is the rational, reasonable, problem solving part of us, the part which tries to divorce emotion from the irrational, asks questions, recognizes reality for what it is and realizes that where people are concerned, things are not always black and white.

TA is not an all-encompassing solution to our communication needs. TA is nothing more than a tool that is available to us. The techniques, once learned, can become instinctive in helping us see ourselves and those with whom we communicate more clearly and, when necessary, more rationally.

ENDNOTES

1. Eric Berne, *Transactional Analysis in Psychotherapy: A Systematic Individual and Social Psychiatry,* (New York), Grove Press, 1961.

2. Mayo and Jarvis, *The Psychology of Leisure Travel,* CBI Publishing, Foreword, 1981

CHAPTER 7

LIFE POSITIONS

The TA LIFE POSITION Model

In addition to coming from an EGO STATE - PARENT, ADULT or CHILD, we are usually seen as coming from (or living in) a certain *LIFE POSITION*.[1] The EGO STATE is of the moment; the LIFE POSITION is more long-term, developed over a period of time, the characteristic way we have come to look at others and the world in general.

In TA terms, each of us carries a generalized feeling about ourselves:

I'm OKAY

or

I'm NOT OKAY

We also have generalized feelings about others:

YOU'RE OKAY

or

YOU'RE NOT OKAY

The Four LIFE POSITIONS

The view of reality which develops then places us in one of four categories (or LIFE POSITIONS) as follows:

1. I'M OKAY - YOU'RE OKAY

2. I'M OKAY - YOU'RE NOT OKAY

3. I'M NOT OKAY - YOU'RE OKAY

4. I'M NOT OKAY - YOU'RE NOT OKAY

Our constitutional makeup, energy level, intelligence and general health help determine our LIFE POSITION. Just as important, or more so, say the TA theorists, are the emotional experiences encountered while growing up. Emotional experiences are recorded in the brain and leave permanent marks. In TA terms, these marks are called TAPES, providing a "life script" from which we play out our lives. Although these tapes cannot be erased, they can be modified or "updated," based on changes that occur in our environment.

Another way of saying that tapes are permanent is that we are all programmed by our environment. The biggest things in the child's environment are the parents, later the school teacher, the coach, the minister, the kids around him or her. We are programmed by the school and college attended and by our associates. Early programs remain with us and are replayed. Not only the thoughts are replayed, but the feelings of joy, inferiority, etc., originally experienced. We can, however, make new decisions and break free from the past, at least to an extent. New experiences "rewire" us, as do fresh viewpoints, religious conversion, and, yes, even reading this material. It implies that we are intelligent, rational beings possessing free will and that we are capable of change.

Recognizing which LIFE POSITION is in effect is not easy in guest relations, because we do not usually know our guests well enough to place them accurately in their LIFE POSITION. Some theorists, however, feel that a person can be "pegged" in less than five minutes of conversation.

Perhaps we don't even know our own LIFE POSITION; besides, there are times when almost everyone moves from one LIFE POSITION to another. The four "OKAY models" are useful, however, in that, like the PAC model, they provide a handle or guide for human relations, putting a complicated concept into a neat package.

Before specifically defining the four LIFE POSITIONS, an additional "tool" needs to be introduced which can help us more clearly visualize the LIFE POSITIONS of ourselves and others.

The EGO-GRAM

Tests have been developed whereby each of our EGO states can be synthesized and graphically depicted. Such graphs are known as "EGO-GRAMS." Concept of the EGO-GRAM requires understanding of what might be called our "psychic energy." We all have a "finite amount" of this energy, and the total amount possessed is "distributed" over our various EGO STATES to one degree or another. For example:

Let us assume that whatever psychic energy one possesses is divided into 40 equal units. We then distribute portions of these 40 units against the five ego states shown below.

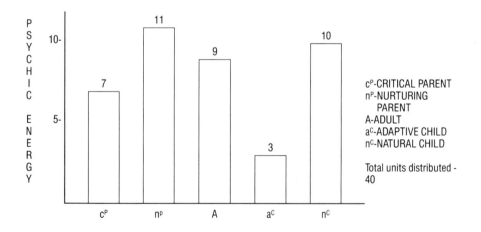

c^p-CRITICAL PARENT
n^p-NURTURING PARENT
A-ADULT
a^c-ADAPTIVE CHILD
n^c-NATURAL CHILD

Total units distributed - 40

Note the distribution: 7 units to the CRITICAL PARENT;
11 units to the NURTURING PARENT
9 units to the ADULT
3 units to the ADAPTIVE CHILD
and   10 units to the FREE (or NATURAL) CHILD.

This particular EGO-GRAM approaches a diagrammatical description of one of our four LIFE POSITION models (I'M OKAY, YOU'RE OKAY).

Those readers interested in a more objective evaluation of their own psychic energy distribution (EGO-GRAM) might enjoy completing the self-evaluation found in APPENDIX C. In this evaluation, you are presented with 75 statements and asked to indicate with a " + " or "-" whether or not the statement is representative of how you feel about a certain issue. A scoring key and conversion table is also provided, which will allow you to convert the information into an EGO-GRAM. Once you complete the evaluation, ask a friend, or someone you consider to be dependable enough to be totally frank, to answer the same questions as though the questions were being asked *about you*. This second evaluation, scored in the same manner, may then be compared with the self-evaluation to see how similarly or differently you may be seen by those with whom you communicate regularly.

Guest relations has its roots in personal communication and how we come across to others. It is, therefore, better advised that we accept the EGO-GRAM created by the evaluation of another person rather than the one created by ourselves.

LIFE POSITIONS Defined

Characteristic assumptions made about ourselves and others in terms of the OKAY models are as follows:

I'M OKAY-YOU'RE OKAY

I like me, I like you. This is the adult-like perspective and presumably the result of a happy childhood and a number of OKAY experiences. "Success breeds success." "I like everything around me. I enjoy what I'm doing. I grow with every new day and am thrilled by the experiences in life." People who spend a majority of their psychic lives in this LIFE POSITION help others through their NURTURING PARENT, enjoy life through a healthy expression of their NATURAL CHILD and succeed in the accomplishment of tasks while in their ADULT. The CRITICAL PARENT and the ADAPTIVE CHILD EGOS in such people are limited to rare expressions during times of unusual stress, emotional fatigue or physical illness. A subjective EGO-GRAM of this LIFE POSITION would appear as follows:

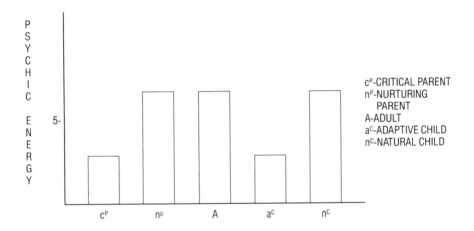

I'M NOT OKAY - YOU'RE OKAY

This LIFE POSITION is the result of experiences carried over from the child development period when "big people" around seemed OKAY but the individual felt puny in comparison. "They" could do everything; the individual could do little. Others were strong, competent, coping; the individual was relatively inadequate. In TA terms, these experiences are "TAPES" carried over into adult life with a feeling load which inhibits joy and self-confidence. In our society, much of what is done is "deficiency motivated", which, in TA terms, is "I'M NOT OKAY- YOU'RE OKAY"; the feeling of inadequacy. Specific characteristics of a person in this life position would be:

Low self-confidence.

Inferiority complex and feelings of inadequacy.

Never right and can never do right.

Always have small problems and in need of help.

Constantly seeking the NURTURING PARENT in others, but most times hooking the CRITICAL PARENT.

The subjective EGO-GRAM of a person in this life position would appear:

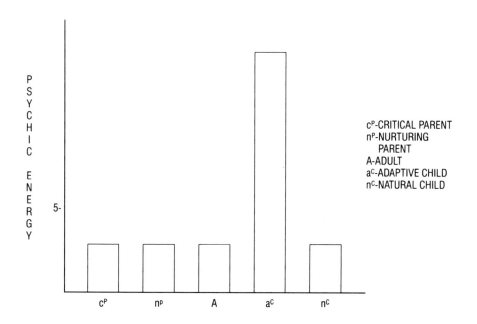

cp-CRITICAL PARENT
np-NURTURING
       PARENT
A-ADULT
ac-ADAPTIVE CHILD
nc-NATURAL CHILD

I'M OKAY - YOU'RE NOT OKAY

Perhaps because of real-life brutality or humiliation from adults, the "TAPES" recorded in growing up and their resultant load of feelings, cause the individual in this LIFE POSITION to be wary, distrustful, perhaps cynical or even vengeful. Since other people have taken advantage of "ME," I will now take advantage of "THEM." A person in this LIFE POSITION comes across as a superior "Mr. Right," quick to play games and put people down. This person has little or no confidence in others and is usually the authority of all that is right. Such persons seldom listen while others are talking, but are constantly thinking about what they will say next. Living predominately in their CRITICAL PARENT EGO, the subjective EGO-GRAM would appear as follows:

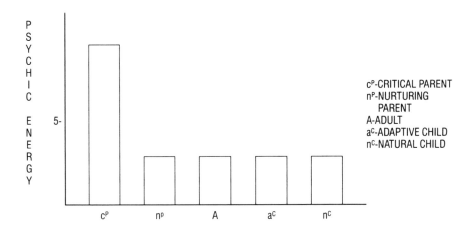

cᴾ-CRITICAL PARENT
nᴾ-NURTURING PARENT
A-ADULT
aᶜ-ADAPTIVE CHILD
nᶜ-NATURAL CHILD

I'M NOT OKAY- YOU'RE NOT OKAY

"I don't like myself, and I don't like you. There is not much either of us can do about it. Life is a drag, something to be endured along with the people who inhabit the world. I am not pleased with myself or with anyone else." Such persons do not trust themselves or other people. They jump from their CRITICAL PARENT to their ADAPTIVE CHILD with confusing regularity, in many cases appearing to be psychologically maladjusted. Many persons living within this LIFE POSITION are either institutionalized, or should be. The resultant EGO-GRAM would then be:

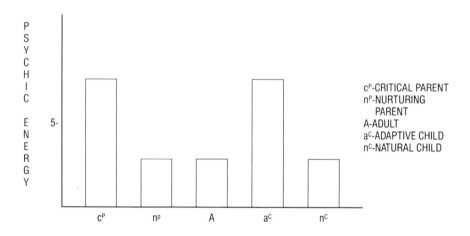

Physical/Mental State, Fatigue and the NOT OKAY Condition

Because the CHILD tapes recorded in the brain carry their load of feelings and are triggered by experiences similar to the original PARENT stimuli, it is easy to understand why everyone from time to time moves into the "I'M NOT OKAY" life position.

Undoubtedly our state of health, blood sugar level and the way we are treated on the job affects our LIFE POSITION. A person with bleeding ulcers can hardly be expected to feel "I'M OKAY." Hearing one's spouse point out our inadequacies can trigger similar "critiques" by parents or teachers that occurred years ago, and can call up the CHILD ego state and an "I'M NOT OKAY" LIFE POSITION. Fears aroused in the past are played back and often "hook" us into an inappropriate ego state and LIFE POSITION.

Summarizing the Four LIFE POSITIONS

I'M OKAY - YOU'RE OKAY

I'M NOT OKAY - YOU'RE OKAY

I'M OKAY - YOU'RE NOT OKAY

I'M NOT OKAY - YOU'RE NOT OKAY

TAPES: Memories of experiences, including the feelings that went with them, which trigger or influence present behavior. TAPES can be "updated," critically examined and their effects on present thinking changed. TAPES can also be analyzed by examining their respective EGO-GRAMS, and it helps us to understand the LIFE POSITIONS of others when we objectively analyze our own EGO-GRAM and LIFE POSITION.

We have reviewed two TA concepts, the EGO STATE and the LIFE POSITION. We see how at a given time a person has a generalized feeling about self and about others (LIFE POSITIONS), and how, during a particular transaction, a person "comes from" one of the three EGO STATES.

ENDNOTES

1. Thomas Harris, *I'm OK - You're OK: A Practical Guide To Transactional Analysis,* (New York: Harper and Row, 1969).

CHAPTER 8

OTHER TA CONCEPTS

Role Playing

Sociologists tell us that we all play roles in life, knowingly or unknowingly. At any given time, the same individual may play the role of parent, businessperson, teacher, lover, dependent, leader, etc. Individuals have dominant roles which they play, but also have latent roles which can be played when the occasion calls for them. These roles are influenced by the TAPES we carry around in our nervous system. At any given time, a supervisor can be playing the role of instructor, bookkeeper, parent, confessor, friend, salesperson or other role. The tenets of TA would have the practitioner develop the role of ADULT especially while on the job. They would sensitize the practitioner to the person's own role and the role of the conversant. Being aware of the roles being played, the individual can change roles appropriately and say the right things to move the other person from one role to another.

The person studying TA can role play by acting out a situation and, in the process, identify where each person in the psychodrama is coming from while noting the ego states involved.

Role playing takes place in any job. Tip employees may enjoy role playing as a way to increase their tips, playing roles in which they play the part called for by the guest. Both parties may be aware of what is going on, the guest playing the role of "Mr. Big" and the employees acting the necessary part indicated, responding to every cue given by the guest. The role can be fun and highly rewarding for all players.

In a restaurant, roles can shift during the course of a meal. After a big night, "Mr. Big" becomes "Mr. Little." He wants to revert to the CHILD role, and says to the server, "Boy, what a meal. Alka Seltzer won't do it." Whereupon the server is supposed to switch roles to become the NURTURING PARENT and say, "You'd better just go home and get a good night's rest."

Psychodrama and role playing have been used for many years in other connections, and are also useful in TA training.

Game Playing

As indicated above, ROLE PLAYING is a TA technique which might be used to determine the EGO STATE a person might be coming from, and can be used to direct conversations and counseling leading to problem solutions. GAME PLAYING is quite a different concept, however.

In TA theory, game playing involves transactions which in some way are "designed to obtain a hidden payoff," i.e., for an ulterior motive.

By classical definition, a "psychological game" is an ongoing series of COMPLEMENTARY-ULTERIOR TRANSACTIONS leading to a predictable outcome. The causes of games are the desire of one participant to gain a payoff by having either their PARENT or CHILD EGO stroked.

According to Maurice F. Villere and associates, games are irrational and unreasonable ways of looking at common everyday situations.[1] They do not support reasonable objectives whether professional or personal, nor do they help morale or cause people to strive for achievement. Games cause insecure feelings to emerge in other people, causing others to mistrust everyone, and games fail to promote good morale or motivate achievement. In addition, games end up by hurting people's feelings, promoting distrust and hampering communications.

In spite of these negative assertions, games are still played for many reasons:

Employees — to avoid doing their jobs.

Guests — to get even for bad experiences.

Managers — to wield power and shrink from responsibility.

Villere and associates indicate that there are five general reasons why people play games.[2]

1. *People seek negative reinforcement — if there is no positive reinforcement available.*

    When perceived rewards are not available, people will set themselves up to be put down. (Game is based in the CHILD.)

2. *NOT-OKAY life positions are breeding grounds for games.*

    If people feel others are trying to get them (perceived or actual), they are likely to indulge in game-playing as a protective device. ("They'll get me if I don't get them first.") (Originates in CHILD; shifts to CRITICAL PARENT.)

3. *Occasionally, people need to demonstrate their superiority.*

    Some people have a need to impress others (ONE-UPMANSHIP). (Originates in the CRITICAL PARENT.)

4. *Games are used to roleplay a gamer's life script.*

    There are usually three roles involved when game playing is based on a life script: "persecutor," "victim" and sometimes a "false rescuer." (Originates in CHILD, shifts to PARENT.)

5. *When boredom sets into a group, a game could result.*

    Excitement can be created by game-playing, even when there is no personal gain to be made. The game becomes its own irrational reward. (May originate in the CHILD, will shift to the PARENT.)

How To Avoid Games

The best way to avoid games is first to be aware of the types of games that can be played. When you recognize that a game is being initiated, get into your ADULT and stay there. Don't let your PARENT or CHILD get "hooked." If that doesn't work, change the subject or, as a last resort, simply walk away.

Some of the Games that People Play

The technique most often used in the cataloging of games is to give them a name representative of the "hidden payoff" intended by their initiator. In the examples that follow, the name of each game will suggest the transactions that constitute the game. All games may be played by anyone so inclined, whether they be guest, service employee, supervisor, manager or top executive.

Guest games usually rely on the institution's belief that the guest is always right (of course they are not), and management's willingness to go to great lengths to keep the customer happy. Guests who are game players will never be satisfied. When the guest is playing games, staff members should never participate. Remember the ADULT EGO, change the subject, call a manager for assistance or simply and politely excuse yourself from the conversation. The following is a compilation of games initially cataloged by Berne in 1964.³ They were given practical application to the hospitality industry by Villere and associates in 1983.⁴ They are presented here with elaboration.

The Exception Game

"AIN'T IT AWFUL"

Recall that this game was mentioned earlier as being the only game in which none of the "participants" are intended to be hurt. AIN'T IT AWFUL is therefore an exception to the rule regarding one of the participants being the target of the ULTE-RIOR TRANSACTION. Specifically, it is played by two or more people, each coming from their CRITICAL PARENT, criticizing a third person, event, happening or thing.

Although it is not appropriate to criticize another, this particular game is one of those most often played to relieve boredom.

Notice how the name of the game suggests the transactions involved in the communications. It should be easy to imagine two people criticizing a third person for an indefinite period of time, with the last transaction of the conversation being a predictable "Ain't it awful!"

Recall, however, that in all other games, one of the participants will be victimized, quite possibly the initiator of the game.

Guest Games

"JUST LOOKING"

This game is played by the guest who has no real intention of buying or "booking," but is continually calling for quotes, rate adjustments and asking questions that seek the limits of complimentary policies. Once this game is recognized, staff members should spend as little time as possible with these game players, as they will monopolize staff time to the detriment of valuable paying guests. Staff members should ask the initiator of such a game to "contact the hotel again once a commitment decision has been concluded," and should excuse themselves from further conversation at that time.

"WHERE ARE THE FREEBIES?"

A variation of "Just Looking" is the game in which guests are continually searching for something for nothing. Whereas the great majority of convention planners are expert and most professional in their dealings with hotels, some might present a problem. It is quite common for large hotel groups to obtain certain "complimentaries" due to the size of the overall piece of business. One free room for every 50 rooms purchased is quite common in the corporate group market segment of hotel occupancies. Occasionally, an inexperienced or unprofessional meeting planner expects his or her coordinating abilities to be measured by how much is received from the facility for nothing. A written "complimentary policy" is usually the best defense against this type of game. The meeting planner is simply shown in writing what the hotel's policy is regarding group complimentaries, which usually ends the game immediately.

This author recalls a hotel group market salesperson who, if pressured by a group meeting planner for a reduction in rate due to the size of the group, cleverly but professionally gave the meeting planner a choice. For example:

Consider the meeting planner who wanted 90 percent of the hotel's guest rooms in high season at a 25 percent reduction in room rate. The meeting planner's argument would usually be based on the outstanding piece of business being brought into the hotel. "Rates, dates or space" the hotel sales manager would reply, indicating that the meeting planner could select two of the three variables. He, the sales manager, would pick the third. The meeting planner was quick to reply, "Okay, I'll take 90 percent of your rooms and a 25 percent reduction from rack rate." "Fine," said the sales manager, "We will book you on December 24."

Another variation of this game might be called, "WE DESERVE A REBATE." The staff member should be wary of the guest who, from the beginning of a visit, is continually finding something wrong with the service, the food, the staff, the rooms, etc. This is a good indication that a request for "adjustment" of the guest's bill will be forthcoming. The answer to this game is to make sure that there is nothing wrong with the service, lest you become involved with the next game.

"NOW I'VE GOT YOU (You Son of a Bitch)"

Abbreviated "NIGYSOB," this particular game has many variations, all of which lead to the ulterior conclusion - "vengeance."

When played by guests, this game usually results from

unrealistic and excessive expectations. To counteract this impression, personnel must always portray their facility in a balanced fashion so guests won't dwell on one particular shortcoming. When a hotel advertises "We've got the cleanest rooms in town," they had better be. It would be better to have the cleanest rooms in town, and allow guests to make their own judgment based on a more objective observation.

"TAKE ME TO THE MANAGER"

Assuming that the employee is capable of resolving a problem if allowed to, this game proclaims an obvious attempt to intimidate the service employee. The best way to defuse this game is to take the person directly to the manager without any resistance. The fun of this game is in upsetting the staff.

"UPROAR"

When the guest plays UPROAR, the game may take two different forms - the steady stream of complaints or the sudden outburst and attempted argument. Arguing with a game player is pointless, since the player gets strokes from the argument. The service employee should remain calm until the UPROAR is complete, then engage the guest in a discussion designed to resolve the problem while avoiding imagined or unreasonable complaints made by the guest. Although a complaint may be completely justified, UPROAR is not conducive to problem solving and only serves to delay corrective action being taken.

Manager Games

"BLEMISH"

Managers can be great initiators of games in their unique positions of being able to force their games on others. Managers make policy and describe rules - so, if managing out of a NOT OKAY position, games may result. BLEMISH is a good example. Sometimes called "Let's Sweat the Small Stuff," "Blemish" is a game of trivia based on the manager spending a majority of time reviewing reports, inventory controls, details, etc. This is not active management but a retreat to a safe area. This manager usually finds fault but never provides direction.

"MANAGERIAL NIGYSOB"

When played by managers, NIGYSOB is sometimes coined, "Bet you can't get around this one." Usually originating from the CRITICAL PARENT, the game might have one of the following scenarios:

1. Setting overly high objectives to provide ammunition for criticism and attack when the employee fails. ("What, no thousand sales calls today?")

2. Failing to give employees the wherewithal to do a good job. The manager might say to the housekeeper, "Your room attendants have been doing a lousy job in cleaning the rooms. You'd better get them on the ball, and soon!" Ideally, the housekeeper can objectively, and from the ADULT, point out the substandard and worn-out vacuum cleaners that the staff may have been provided to work with.

2. Managers pushing packages that won't sell, or failing to create ones that do.

3. Criticizing an employee after the fact, rather than providing guidance during an activity.

4. Telling employees to specifically behave one way, then criticizing them for not acting another.

These tactics cause trouble and encourage employees to play the same type of game against the manager.

Some NIGYSOB gamers may not be too clear about their motives. Suppose an employee wishes to seriously embarrass another. In the hearing of the manager, the employee comments, "It seems strange that every time Joe is on my shift, guest complaints go up."

The transaction ostensibly came from the ADULT - but it actually came from the CHILD. The ulterior motive is that of putting Joe on the spot.

"MANAGERIAL UPROAR"

Not only capable of being played by the guest or anyone who perceives himself or herself as having the upper hand, "Uproar" is often played by managers. This game also has several other names, such as "Whom Can I Attack First," or "Gripe, Gripe, Gripe."

Goals or performance are never good enough. Consider the morning phone calls to the subordinate, in which the manager continues asking questions about yesterday's business. Continues, that is, until the subordinate can't answer one of them, then comes the barrage of criticism from the manager.

Employees as Game-Players

"IF IT WEREN'T FOR YOU"

This is a game whereby the initiator is continually blaming someone else for the results of actions. Imagine these scenarios:

"If it weren't for your being on my back all the time, I wouldn't make these mistakes."

"If it weren't for your nagging, I would feel more like being polite to the guests."

"If it weren't for your being late, I wouldn't be behind in my orders."

"If it weren't for your bugging me, I wouldn't come in late."

Other Classic Games

Having covered the dialogue of several classical games, only the names of games should now be needed for the reader to visualize the transactions involved. Read the following names of games and imagine the dialogue.

"CORNERED"

(Heads you lose, tails you lose.) Giving assignments that

can never be met.

"WELL, I WAS ONLY TRYING TO HELP"

(Allows the manager to become a "false rescuer").

"LET'S YOU AND HIM FIGHT"

(Played by the individual who encourages conflict between two subordinates so that the initiator can become a false rescuer.) A situation is created whereby a healthy striving for excellence is undermined by an unhealthy competition for the favor of a superior.

"THE ANALYST"

Some people fancy themselves as psychologists. "Didn't you love your mother? I believe that basically being an insecure person is what's interfering with your good performance." Untrained psychologists may do much more harm than good.

"DROP BACK AND PUNT"

In this game, the manager abdicates management responsibility. Responsibilities are passed onto subordinates. This person has "retired" but failed to tell the paymaster.

"POOR ME"

(Played from the ADAPTIVE CHILD.)

"AFTER ALL I'VE DONE FOR YOU"
(Out to hook the guilt in the ADAPTIVE CHILD.)

CHILD to CHILD Games

Many games are played CHILD to CHILD. The bouncy young sales person is full of fun and eager for a little social companionship, or more. "Hey, it's a beautiful night; too beautiful for you to be tied up here all evening."

The attractive employee, flattered, says, "Oh, I agree, but I'm not off until midnight."

"What is there to do around here other than eat, drink and watch TV?"

"That depends on what you have in mind."

"Oh, I might have a lot of things in mind."

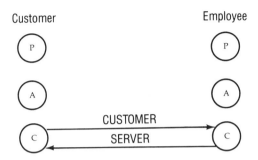

The CHILD is hooked to CHILD and a pleasant little game is progressing: It may be fun and it may be legitimate, but it could give the establishment a bad reputation. The CHILD is stroking the CHILD, which is fine, but it takes sensitivity on the part of the employee to avoid causing hard feelings or being labeled a teaser, unless the employee is indeed interested and wants to continue the mating game. In that case, the employee had best be refreshed on the rules of the hotel regarding fraternization with the guests.

Some men and women play the manipulative controlling CHILD in such situations, feeling a sense of power in outsmarting the other person, titillating, tantalizing, offering tidbits for no other reason than the enjoyment of watching the other person wiggle and reach.

"I notice you are wearing a wedding ring," the moralizing PARENT speaking, after having led the person on.

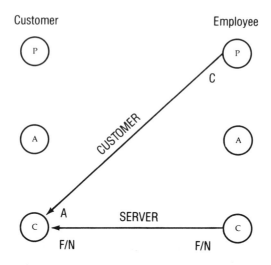

In this example, the game just changed from "LET'S TEASE EACH OTHER" to "NIGYSOB."

The manipulative person is adept at the ulterior transaction, saying one thing and implying another, or directing the thoughts of the other person without the person knowing it. The *manipulator* may not even be aware of what is being done.

Guest: "Which room do you recommend?"

Employee: "The lanai suites are beautiful."

Guest: "They are also overpriced."

Employee: "Yes, they are expensive. Few can afford them."

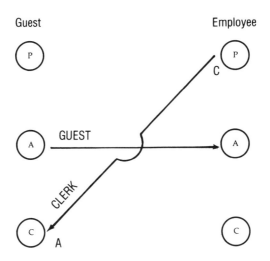

The employee, perhaps even without knowing it, is moralizing, but is also playing the ulterior game of trying to influence the guest to buy the most expensive item - by making the guest feel inferior if the suite is not bought. The employee is "talking down," playing PARENT and talking to the CHILD of the guest.

The transaction is ULTERIOR in that the employee has tried to "hook" the CHILD in the guest, PARENT to CHILD.

If the CHILD is hooked, the guest may react:

"Oh, I can afford one. I'll take a suite."

On the other hand, the PARENT in the guest may resent the insinuation that he or she cannot afford the suite, and make a "superior" condescending statement, such as: "Don't get smart with me, young man; tell the manager to come here." Or, the guest can respond as an ADULT, and ignore the comment, choosing a room based on objective selection criteria.

Game playing goes on at all levels of society and in business. Some people become adept at immediately putting others on the defensive or in a subordinate position. Hitler and Mussolini did so by placing themselves behind huge desks and surrounding themselves with aides, guards and the panoply of power. Driving the prestige car, owning the imposing home, dressing in the latest fashion is, in part, game playing, designed to impress others and place the player in the superior role.

In guest relations, game playing can boomerang and lose the guest completely. The temptation may be to "one-up" the game player. Like winning an argument, the end result of one-upping the other person can be negative feelings all around.

If a guest starts game playing, the employee can simply refuse to take part in the game by remaining silent, or by changing the subject.

Life is much simpler, especially in guest relations, when transactions are kept "up front," open, honest and straightforward.

ACTIVE LISTENING (A Form of Directed Counseling)

Active listening is yet another TA technique whereby we as counselors may become more objective in our relations with people. At the same time, active listening can prevent others from manipulating us by transferring their burdens to our shoulders. It is a better way to allow the NURTURING PARENT to flourish rather than to accept the burdens of others. When we accept the burdens of others as our own, we destroy an opportunity for the other person to learn to solve his or her own problems.

In his book *"P.E.T., Parent Effectiveness Training"* Thomas Gordon[5] defines ACTIVE LISTENING as your giving feedback in the feelings you hear another person expressing. It allows them to see how you have interpreted what they said. ACTIVE LISTENING is a technique which conveys a message of "I care," or "I'm concerned about you." ACTIVE LISTENING is also a clinical technique developed to help a frustrated person overcome emotional blocks.

The average emotionally upset employee will start to complain to a supervisor and then suddenly reach a dead end. For example, the employee may say, "That Joe is just plain lazy; he won't do his job and the rest of us have to carry his share of the load. It's just not fair!" At this point the employee hits a psychological block. But it is apparent that all of the frustration has not been drained off and the supervisor needs to build a bridge to further communication. The supervisor needs to remove the emotional roadblock that has stopped this catharsis before it is complete. This is accomplished by "feeding back" — after the employee has reached a dead end — the final feelings of the employee.

In this case, the supervisor may feed back an understanding of the employee's feelings by saying, *"You don't feel Joe is assuming his fair part of the job."* This feedback of the employee's feelings tends to build a bridge or remove the psychological block enabling the employee to continue to express the aggressive hostility and get it out of his or her system. The employee may now go on with, "That's right! And another thing. He never comes in on time, and he wants Pete or me to cover up for him. But I told him yesterday, I won't do it, not anymore. He can either get in on time or take the consequences," and perhaps at this point another roadblock is reached. Now again, the supervisor feeds back a reflected feeling — *"You feel Joe is shirking his responsibilities."* Again this removes a roadblock and the employee can continue.

In this example, the supervisor is putting emphasis on the feelings of the employee, but in a very ADULT way.

Summarizing from the above example:

1. The supervisor shows caring by "listening" to what the employee is saying.

2. The supervisor confirms this caring by actively giving feedback on what the employee was heard to say.

3. As long as the employee is talking, the supervisor does not interrupt.

4. When the supervisor does give feedback, it is given by reflecting the "feelings" being expressed by the employee. This tends to help the employee overcome a psychological roadblock to further communications.

5. The technique continues until all feelings of hostility have been vented, at which time the employee should be able to arrive at a workable solution to his or her own problem.

6. The supervisor's statements do not suggest answers, only ADULT understanding of feelings.

Care must be exercised in using the techniques of ACTIVE LISTENING to ensure that all feedback comes from the ADULT, and does not suggest an answer to the problem. The answer must come from the person with the problem.

EXERCISE 3

PRACTICE IN ACTIVE LISTENING

For each statement, choose the response that seems to exhibit the most productive use of active listening. Also, see if you can identify the EGO STATES from which each response is coming.

1. I've been working on this report for over two weeks, and now Miller says the whole project's been canceled.

   a. That's pretty disappointing.

   b. You spent all that time on the lousy report and now the whole thing is canned!

   c. I worked on the project, too, you know!

   d. It would have been better had Miller told you sooner.

2. I really like my job. I mean, I wouldn't want to be at it for the rest of my life; but then, you can't start at the top.

   a. If you had your way, you'd be president of the company.

   b. You think you're doing okay for a beginner, eh?

   c. I get the feeling you're not altogether satisfied.

   d. Sounds like you'd welcome a challenge.

3. It's not that I don't think it's a good idea. It's just that it's never been done before and I, for one, prefer to stick to the tried and true.

   a. There's nothing wrong with the old way of doing things.

   b. If a person always jumps on the wagon just because it's the thing to do, it'd be a real mess.

   c. You feel rather hesitant about making a change.

   d. Nothing ventured, nothing gained.

4. I'll do it if I have to, but this is the third time this week that you've given me something extra to do. Not that I mind, but I'm still not through typing those other letters you gave me.

   a. You think I should give this assignment to someone else.

   b. You're beginning to feel swamped.

   c. You don't have time to do this one.

   d. You wish I'd get off your back.

5. I don't care what the department says. I just got these figures last night and I'm not about to give them an answer until I've had a chance to study the numbers.

   a. They're being pretty demanding.

   b. They don't understand how much work you have to do.

   c. You feel they're being pretty unreasonable.

   d. I know just how you feel.

6. I just heard that our new product is being pushed back another month. Here we go again.

   a. What's that going to do to our customers?

   b. Sounds like you had a lot riding on meeting the old schedule.

   c. Oh, joy!

   d. After all the work we've done.

7. I can't believe Harold didn't know about the promotion in advance. He spent half of his time over in that other department. But I'm not about to connive my way to the top.

   a. It's not what you know, it's who you know.

   b. You don't feel Harold deserved the promotion?

   c. You don't approve of his methods?

d. The only way to get ahead in this business is to play their game.

The Boss Actively Listens (a Scenario)

Being a service employee is a demanding job if done well. It is often less well paid than comparable jobs in other industries. Relations between employees can become strained. The TA approach in directed counseling can be helpful here as well. Put yourself in the place of this supervisor and see how TA might be used.

A typical interaction between supervisor and employee: The employee comes in asking for a raise. "Mr. Big, I have now been here for three months and I feel I am doing as good or a better job than Mary Jones, who I hear is getting 50 cents an hour more than I am, and I would like a raise."

Mr. Big thinks to himself, "This cry baby is late every third day, is indifferent to customers, sometimes rude, makes mistakes in bills and I would let him go now if I could get somebody else to replace him."

Instead of saying as much, which would be letting out the CHILD (and could be quite satisfying for the moment), Mr. Big thinks to himself. "Although all of that is true, I would like to handle this from the ADULT. The purpose of this conversation is to change the employee's behavior."

So he says, "You have been here a while and you feel you are entitled to a raise."

"Yes, I have been doing my best, though I do make a few mistakes now and then."

"You feel that you have been doing your best, but are not always completely accurate in your work."

Already the employee senses that at least Mr. Big is attentive and is reacting to him; it may be what he wanted in the first place.

"Yes, I realize that I don't know the job completely yet, but that takes time; and sometimes I don't really enjoy coming to work."

"You feel that not liking the work could be responsible for your being late once in awhile."

"Yes, it's possible. I hadn't thought of it that way."

"I wonder what could be done to make the job more interesting for you?"

"Well, I don't dislike the job. There are times when I hate like heck to be on the job with Mr. Snide, who is always putting me down when I make some little mistake."

"Well then, it is possible that the reason you don't like the work is the person you work with?"

"Yes, that could be part of it."

The supervisor has allowed the employee to vent some of his antagonism and to see one reason why he is not more pleased with the work and a possible cause for his tardiness and errors.

"You feel Mr. Snide is not too friendly and enjoys rubbing in your lack of experience."

"Yes, that's for sure."

The discussion could now be led around to ways of improving the job, the possibility of changing the shift to work with someone else, the possibility of talking with Mr. Snide and getting his help in training the employee.

The supervisor is not necessarily trying to avoid the issue of a wage increase. He is trying to allow the employee to perceive for himself reasons he is not doing better, and to decide for himself behavior changes necessary to be more effective on the job. The supervisor may be well aware of the real problems, but should avoid coming from the PARENT which may trigger the CHILD and reinforce a PARENT-CHILD relationship that may be already started.

The ideal employee is self-directed, self motivated and creative, perceiving the necessary changes and eager to improve his or her work and the overall business.

The PARENT is forever ready to jump in and tell people what to do; the ADULT says, "Hey now, let's wait awhile, let's talk this over, let's see if we can get the other person to see for himself or herself what is needed, even though it may not be the very same thing that my ADULT sees as necessary."

The PARENT expects instant obedience; the ADULT recognizes that self-motivation is much slower, but more meaningful and lasting.

ENDNOTES

1. Maurice F. Villere, et al., *Games Nobody Wins*, Cornell H.R.A. Quarterly, (Ithaca, New York, November, 1983,) pp. 72-79.

2. Maurice F. Villere, et al., *ibid.*, p. 75.

3. Eric Berne, (*op. cit.*, 1964).

4. Maurice F. Villere, et al., *op. cit.*, pp. 75-79.

5. Thomas Gordon, *P.E.T.: Parent Effectiveness Training,* Wyden Press, 1975.

CHAPTER 9

TA AT WORK

Stroking

TA presents some new buzz words. "Stroking" is one such word, and refers to saying or doing things which reinforce an EGO STATE. In many cases, strokes soothe, flatter and reassure the other person; in other cases, they may scold, warn or threaten.

In human development, physical stroking precedes and sets the stage for psychological stroking. The parent cuddles the infant, providing a deep sense of security, warmth and love. Implying recognition, verbal strokes are usually sought early in childhood development. "Positive strokes" are the most encouraging to growth. "Negative strokes" are better than none at all. The absence of strokes, however, is usually crippling.

Infants have been known to die for lack of stroking; adults cannot be healthy without it. As we mature, we learn to accept substitutes for the original physical contact. Sex relations present the opportunity for intense psychological reassurance for both parties. Words and gestures are substitutes for the touching and physical contact. Reassurance, approval, reinforcement. Every day and possibly every hour, stroking continues. Stroking is nothing new. It's making the other person pleased with him or herself, or at least recognized as some form of being.

THE FIVE BASIC STROKES

The POSITIVE STROKE

A positive stroke gives information about a person's competence and acceptance. Positive strokes can take many forms and meanings. The obvious Dale Carnegie approach is to flatter people, making them feel better about themselves and, therefore, better about you. TA is more sophisticated, recognizing that both parties benefit psychologically from giving and receiving positive strokes. Positive strokes should not be used as a means of seeking advantage, but as a means of maintaining health and well-being. And they must be genuine. Positive strokes should be used to convey belief that a person is "OKAY." Problem solving is expedited by positive stroking. Creating a condition of trust and liking in an organization sets the stage for innovation and problem solving, breaks down the barriers of suspicion and self-interest, creates good will and opens the channels of communication. Positive strokes are compliments, giving a person a warm feeling, hence the nickname: a positive stroke is known as "a warm fuzzy."

The RITUAL STROKE

This is a much used form of positive stroke having its roots in expectation rather than fact. How many times does one say "Good morning" when, in fact, it is not a good morning? Probably every service job has some insincere elements involved, in the sense that we are called upon to exhibit interest in people in whom it is difficult to have interest. Love the unlovely. Help the obstinate. Listen to the whiner. Stroke the naughty child. Smile at the tyrant. All very difficult to do. But a necessary challenge. All stroking cannot be done with sincerity, but we can try. We should not, however, try to the point that we become phonies or injure our self-respect. There are lines that must be drawn when using the RITUAL STROKE.

The CONDITIONAL STROKE

The conditional stroke is a positive stroke, provided the

recipient meets certain criteria. Fail to meet the condition and the stroke becomes either negative, or no stroke at all. With the conditional stroke, both parties understand the stroke is given with strings attached. The teacher tells the class, "Everyone be on time for the test tomorrow and you won't have to do the last problem." "You do your job and I'll smile at you and pat you on the back," is the understanding which results when a stroke is given with conditions attached. "Shine your shoes" (and Mommy will smile and love you).

"Make your bank balance and I will be your friendly supervisor." "Don't be late for work and we will enjoy coffee together." Conditional strokes partake of game playing, whereas unconditional strokes can be distributed widely with no strings attached. The fact that you are a guest in my place of business is more than enough for me to want to help you, to be friendly and cheerful, to be polite.

The NEGATIVE STROKE

A negative stroke is basically a scolding; an insult, giving one the feeling of being "NOT OKAY." The negative stroke might even be in the form of physical punishment or abuse. The NEGATIVE STROKE is most prevalent when the CRITICAL PARENT is coming on against the ADAPTIVE CHILD. Negative as it may be, it is still a form of recognition and better than no recognition at all. It is nicknamed "the cold prickly."

The PLASTIC STROKE

This stroke has its basis in the ULTERIOR TRANSACTION. It appears to be a positive stroke in all rights, but it is not genuine and, unlike the RITUAL STROKE, has an ulterior hidden meaning. The PLASTIC STROKE may come in the form of a put-down or belated insult. For example: Mary is an employee of the hotel. She dresses as well as can be expected on her salary but, in order to save money for school, is known to get most of her clothes at a thrift shop. One day Mary comes to work in a dress she had not worn before. Jean, in front of several other employees and guests, comments, "Mary, what a lovely dress. Is that one of those you picked up at the Salvation Army?" As ulterior as this stroke is, it is still better than no stroke at all.

All "games" contain PLASTIC STROKING.

How People Work For Strokes

Here is an example of the stroke demand hierarchy at work which shows how the wrong behavior can get more strokes, even though negative, than the right behavior:

Of five sales people who work for one manager, four turn in sales reports on time every week. The other sales person consistently turns in late reports, week after week, month after month. In this situation, it is obvious that the delinquent performance is most likely to get the most attention. The person who produced what the manager didn't want (late data) ended up getting the most strokes. Granted, they were negative — a bawling out, exasperated glances and nagging — but they were strokes.

On the other hand, what kind of recognition was given to the four sales people who supplied the needed information without any prodding? They got neither positive nor negative strokes from the boss, who was preoccupied with late reports. The result was that gradually the pattern changed. One by one, the four reliable sales people began to turn their reports in late, or with obvious mistakes, because "it didn't seem to make any difference."

Six months later, the sales manager could be heard, complaining at the executive staff meeting, "I don't know what happened; I used to be able to count on four of my people, but now, everybody's late." Of course, what happened is that the manager reinforced undesirable behavior by giving it all the attention.

Guest Stroking

Guest-contact persons stroke when they show respect for the other person. They maintain the I'M OKAY position by showing respect, not necessarily deference. The motivation behind the person giving the strokes makes the difference and reflects the LIFE POSITION of the stroker, as well as the person being stroked. Being friendly, outgoing and ready to help suggests I'M OKAY and YOU'RE OKAY. If games are played, in order to place the other person at a disadvantage, the I'M OKAY changes to I'M NOT OKAY and don't really want to help you, only take advantage of you.

The guest, often tired and frustrated, may have a greater stroke hunger than normal. "I'M NOT OKAY, YOU'RE OKAY, stroke me."

What makes the transaction delicate is that the I'M NOT OKAY person may demand attention and compliments, yet conclude that the giver is out to get something. The "I'M OKAY - YOU'RE OKAY" LIFE POSITION recognizes that positive strokes are essential for well-being and the healthy person receives them as legitimate.

Strokes All Around

Much of life is spent seeking strokes - reassurance that we are valued, respected people, liked and wanted by others. Part of the motivation for inviting others to our home is to give and to get strokes. The situation is supposed to be non-competitive, comfortable and stroke-inducing. Successful social hosts see to it that everyone in the group is stroked so that all leave feeling relaxed and liking themselves and others in the group.

The Stroke Emporium

Business settings are suited for stroking, some more than others. A major reason for shopping is the expectation of receiving "good service," meaning that employees will be solicitous and responsive to the guest's mood, and that the establishment will be non-competitive and comfortable. The guest usually wants to be served by an "I'M OKAY - YOU'RE OKAY" kind of person who accepts and responds to him or her.

A dining room and bar can be considered a stroke emporium, an ego haven where the guest has the ego refreshed and reinforced, an ego massage parlor where guest-contact employees are the masseurs and masseuses.

Why does anyone prefer one establishment over another? The appointments, yes; the products, yes; the convenience, yes; but also the ambience, the concern offered, the friendliness, the cheerfulness and the stroking provided.

The mechanics of greeting and serving are important, but should be done as unobtrusively as possible, with maximum efficiency, so that time can be had for stroking. Strokes all around, for guests and for fellow employees. Why not? Stroking costs nothing. It can call for a great deal of ingenuity and subtlety, and is a constant challenge. Strokes beget strokes. I like you; you like me. I stroke you; you stroke me.

Stroking is not necessarily flattery or making vapid remarks about the person's dress, skin color, new shoes, diction, handwriting, etc. It can be simple, active, responsive listening which the ADULT is controlling. It is asking questions in a well-mannered way. "May I be of help?" NEVER: "What can I do for you?" Never talking down or acting superior or supercilious. Always acting responsibly, courteously and with dignity.

Can stroking be overdone? Obviously, yes, especially when done in a phony (plastic) manner that suggests the stroker is not really interested, is lying or is seeking an advantage. It is surprising how most of us respond to praise, to attention and interest, even when laid on with a heavy trowel. Disraeli, the famous prime minister of England during Victorian times, was notorious for his lavish use of stroking and made no bones about it. Stroking becomes "charming" if done with taste, discrimination and intelligence. The great courtesans and courtiers of history were confirmed, highly-skilled strokers. Every charming person is actually aware of stroking and of its influence on people and events. The astute stroker is exercising the ADULT, perhaps using a bit of the CHILD and avoiding at all costs the CRITICAL PARENT.

Stroking Techniques

Now that we have two models to refer to, the PAC model and the LIFE POSITION model, we can relate to the guest as having generalized feelings toward others; the LIFE POSITION. In any given transaction, we see the guest as "coming from" the PARENT (CRITICAL or NURTURING), CHILD (ADAPTIVE, FREE or REBEL) or ADULT.

Who Originates, Who Responds

Studies have been conducted of transactions between two people that show that the originator of transactions tends to control and guide the thinking of the transactions that follow. When it is necessary to dominate or control a situation, the service employee should, therefore, originate the transaction, if possible. Other situations may call for response rather than initiation. People who want to make themselves agreeable know when to originate and when to respond. They sense what the situation calls for - origination or response. When a number of guests are waiting for service or when there is a lot of action, the employee should step in, take charge, originate and control.

The Employee Has the Ball

In opening guest transactions, the employee has the ball and is usually expected to guide the transactions. The guest, no matter how successful, dynamic or how potent a leader, may expect the employee to take the lead in the formal transactions that take place in the initial or opening transaction.

SPECIAL STROKING CONSIDERATIONS

When the PARENT is Needed

The PARENT may be appropriate in a number of situations. A man falls unconscious. People welcome instructions from someone who displays confidence and knowledge.

An employee might take charge and say:

"Please let the gentleman lie flat, and let's raise his legs so that the blood will return to his head. Please don't crowd; give him breathing room."

Customers often assume the CHILD role in asking:

"Where can I find a good restaurant?" Such questions are usually from the FREE CHILD and are looking for the NURTURING PARENT who has the answers. (The tone of voice, posture and gestures, however, might be coming from the ADULT.)

Stroking from the NURTURING PARENT

A customer, after a long drive, weary from the highway, stops at a roadside coffee shop, anticipating relief from the glare of the sun and the noise of the highway, able at last to remove herself from the cramped position in the driver's seat. The host can well call forth the guest's CHILD by coming from her NURTURING PARENT.

"I'll bet you're tired from driving."

The woman sighs, "Yes, it has been a long day, and I look forward to a nice meal."

"You might want to relax in the bar before dinner."

Or, Customer: "Is there any place around here where I can get my oil changed?"

NURTURING PARENT: "Just leave the keys to your car here and I'll have Tony come over and pick up the car. It will be ready for you in about two hours."

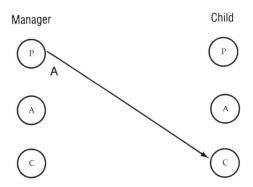

The dining room lends itself to transactions coming from the NURTURING PARENT. Food, for many people, represents the love and affection received as a child, food taken around the family table with Mom and Dad. Mom served not only food but sympathy and security. By association, food took on the same qualities.

In a way, the waitperson can substitute for Mom, providing approval and good will. Often, the guest enters the dinner house as a kind of haven from the world of work. The servers could come from the NURTURING PARENT:

"I'll bet it was a long day. Let me seat you in a nice quiet corner."

The guest drops into a chair and readily accepts the CHILD role:

"Boy, am I tired."

"Could I get you a cool drink before you order?"

There are many situations in which the employee might well come from the NURTURING PARENT:

The guest says plaintively, "I've been waiting 15 minutes for someone to take my order."

Employee: "Oh, I'm sorry. I'll hurry up your order." Or, "I'm sorry for the delay. You must be tired of waiting. I'll give your order special attention."

The NURTURING PARENT may be appropriate for children of all ages, including the old grouch, age 72, who says: "You girls only want to wait on the young guys."

"Oh, come on, sir, you look young to me."

All the grouch may want is personal attention, not unlike the child who feels ignored.

Mothers may need the NURTURING PARENT as much as anyone. Think of the mother who appears at the dining room entrance with the irritable child.

"Johnny is tired of traveling and also a little carsick."

Server: "If his stomach is a little queasy, maybe some tea with milk will settle it. I can get some right away while you relax."

The 200-pounder can easily slip into the CHILD role:

"I can hardly read this fine print."

NURTURING EMPLOYEE: "I'm sorry. Let me read it for you."

A clever variation of this example might occur when the server, sensing that the patron might have a good sense of humor but forgot to bring his glasses, might say: "Here, try mine (as she takes off her own glasses, and passes them to the customer). I have trouble with fine print too." (a CHILD to CHILD variation).

To the hotel guest who complains about having to wait, even though a reservation was made:

"I'm sorry for the delay. Some of our departing guests were a little late in checking out, but our housekeeper will soon have your room ready for you. In the meantime, let me invite you into the restaurant for a complimentary cup of coffee or tea while you wait. I'll come and get you when your room is ready." (What a nice way to start out a visit for a guest when things don't go quite right- by showing a genuine concern.)

The NURTURING PARENT is probably, in part, instinctual, that part of us that protects the weak, loves babies and cuddly animals, wants to help others, feels sympathy and enjoys lending a hand. Without the NURTURING PARENT, there might not be any civilization. Various cultures emphasize one or another of the EGO STATES: some foster cooperation; others encourage competition. In some societies, women are supposed to nurture, men to fight. Within families, one EGO STATE is stressed over another.

The CRITICAL PARENT Strokes the CHILD

There are many situations when the employee's CRITICAL PARENT is sorely tempted to emerge: reprimanding, scolding, moralizing, chastising, talking down to the CHILD.

Guest: "I've got to have some sugar substitute because of my weight problem."

CRITICAL PARENT: "We don't have sugar substitutes. If you really need it, you should bring it with you."

Since we all have PARENT tapes recorded while growing up, the PARENT is always there, waiting to emerge any time we open our mouths without thinking. It is the voice of society, ready to judge, shaping our values, ready to tell others what to do and what is correct. Too often, we come from the PARENT at the wrong time and for the wrong reason. The CRITICAL PARENT is completely inappropriate in the business world and usually inappropriate in guest relations.

It is also easy for a supervisor to turn on the CRITICAL PARENT tape, playing "Big Daddy" or "Big Mommy" to the employee's CHILD.

"So you're late again. Can't you ever be on time? You know, they have alarm clocks to wake people up."

"You say Jane Smith just got a raise and why can't you? Why can't you be like Jane? You ought to shape up and get on the ball if you want a raise."

The CRITICAL PARENT is seldom wanted around a service establishment. Employees in sales and service are not there to correct anyone, modify attitudes, teach anything. Mostly they are there to relate to the guest in an adult way, trying to provide something valued by the guest. Guests should be made comfortable, not uncomfortable. The guest-contact employee is not there to check on people's morals, admonish wrongdoers or decide what is right or wrong about them.

A Place for the CRITICAL PARENT

Once in a while, the employee may need to come from the CRITICAL PARENT. Children of hotel or restaurant guests may decide to use the place of business as a "romp and play" area. Should the employee show signs of being conciliatory, the children who may have been trained to react to the CRITICAL PARENT will take it as a sign of weakness. This can be dangerous, in that they see the employee as someone to bait or chide, or with whom they can play the smart aleck. Firm father or mother figures who give not the slightest suggestion of being friendly or vacillating may be what are needed.

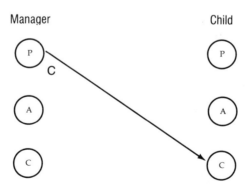

The same stance may be needed with grownups who are cutting up or who are slightly drunk and want to play. Like children, they may be talking loudly to call attention to themselves. A conciliatory attitude may be the wrong approach, an invitation to badger the employee. The best approach may be to come on strong with the stern PARENT:

"You are bothering our other guests. Please quiet down!"

If someone in the group takes this as a challenge, you might try holding to the PARENT position for a time. It is surprising, though, how some relatively young people can take on the CRITICAL PARENT role and quickly hook the CHILD in others. The PARENT is usually more acceptable coming from an older, dignified person.

Handling the Intoxicated Guest

If a person becomes intoxicated, service personnel should call management. Dealing with any inebriated person is a real challenge for the TA-oriented person. That person still has the three EGO STATES, CHILD, PARENT, ADULT, each of which can be tapped or hooked by the right type of stroking. By definition, alcohol tends to wash out the ADULT, the reasoning part of the brain and loose the reins of the CHILD. This means that the intoxicated person might better respond to being treated as a CHILD. The danger lies in the fact that the REBEL CHILD may come to the fore, resenting any display of the PARENT and resort to violence on occasion. Intoxicated people can change moods quickly.

Patience with the person who has been drinking is necessary because the (ADULT) thinking processes are depressed by alcohol. Once a bartender, for example, notes that a patron is going overboard, a firm refusal for more drinks is the only option open.

This author has found that a combination of strokes from the NURTURING PARENT, CRITICAL PARENT and ADULT work best with inebriated people, *never* the CHILD.

First, the CRITICAL PARENT to the registered guest, spoken quietly so as not to embarrass the guest:

"Sir, I'm sorry, but in my judgment you have had too much to drink. Our bartender will not be allowed to serve you any more drinks. I must ask you to leave the lounge. For your safety, I will escort you to your room."

From the ADULT: absolute locked-in eye contact.

And from the NURTURING PARENT: "I know how it feels to have one or two too many. I can remember the night when I needed a friend to help me get home."

In a majority of cases, this approach will work well if you maintain good eye contact with the inebriated guest. It is the ADULT way of saying, "I am in charge of this situation." Should this not be enough, then one other stroke might be appropriate:

From the ADULT: "Sir, we consider you to be a valued guest. I do not want to declare you an undesirable person in our hotel and have to evict you from your room. Please respect our house rules and come with me now." (Again, said with ADULT, locked-in eye contact, and with a NURTURING PARENT smile that says "We care.")

ADULT Stroking

Seldom, if ever, will stroking from the ADULT be inappropriate. There will be occasions when things may have to be explained more than once. Here again, the firm ADULT as occasionally modified by the PARENT stroke will more than likely result in solving the great majority of problems in guest or employee relations.

Ordinarily, the employee tries to keep coming from the ADULT, the little person in the head who:

— Keeps cool in all cases.

— Accepts challenges as challenges.

— Seldom blushes, cries or spends much time putting others down.

— Sees life as full of conflicts and compromises but feels that the intelligent person can cope with such things.

194

— Tries to make decisions only after getting the facts.

— Tries to be forthright in dealing with others.

— Before making a decision, calculates the risks involved and tries to forecast the outcome.

— Recognizes that conditions change. Values change. People change. The ADULT expects such changes and adapts.

The TA approach presses the employee to search for reasonable alternatives, to speak calmly and deliberately and to try to reach the other person's ADULT so that ADULT to ADULT transactions can take place.

Care and Feeding of the ADULT

The ADULT needs support and massage to keep alive and well. The healthy mind in the healthy body: proper sleep, balanced life style, moderation in eating and drinking.

The triggering of destructive actions (tapes, in TA terms) is much easier for the person who is ill or fatigued. Most of us can stand only so much tension over a period of time. We must back off and recoup. Some people do it by sleeping 12 hours when they get the chance. Others do it with sports, watching TV, reading a book, walking. Destructive ways of reducing tension, ways which, in the long run, increase it, are excessive use of alcohol, excessive pursuit of the opposite sex, excessive smoking, excessive eating. Food is a sedative which can be easily overused and, when used excessively, only adds to problems.

Schedule health checkups, conserve energies and follow your own peculiar biorhythms carefully so as to keep in step with them rather than fight the natural sequences of energy buildup, energy depletion, action, rest and action. Work with body rhythms rather than against them.

Cooling It

A reliable technique, calming both self and others, is to

speak in a low, controlled voice. Speak deliberately and slowly, even if you have to exaggerate the slow pace. Most of us instinctively respond to a high-pitched voice, interpreting it as excitement, fear, anxiety or loss of control and tend to react in a similar manner. Calmness begets calmness. Confidence breeds confidence. "I'M OKAY - YOU'RE OKAY." In high-tension situations, the employee is expected to take control.

Speaking in a voice that is somewhat lower than normal causes others to have to strain to listen, which tends to drain off some of the emotional pitch from a situation. "Cooling it" can be done in a number of ways:

— Hooking the other person's ADULT: Speaking and acting in such a way that the other person shifts from the CHILD or PARENT to the ADULT.

— What is said and how it is said moves the transaction to a more businesslike, objective and rational form of communication and behavior.

Most of us welcome the NURTURING PARENT at times, and are grateful if the other person is viewed as worthy and respectable.

To repeat: In any tense situation, one of the best techniques for "cooling it" is to act with confidence, speaking calmly and slowly. Exaggerate the slowness if necessary.

What Not To Say

Try to avoid invoking non sequiturs such as:

— "It's the janitor's responsibility."

— "Most people like our place."

— "That's the way it is."

— "It's out of my hands."

— "I just work here."

— "It's beyond my control."

196

— "You'll have to see the manager about that, and (of course) she's not here right now."

SITUATION STROKING

Handling the Out-of-Cash Guest

A guest presents a personal check that does not have an imprinted name, and which is for an amount above what the establishment policy permits to be cashed. What should be said?

"I am not permitted to cash this kind of check. Is it possible for you to pay in cash, or to establish some form of credit that we accept (indicating acceptable credit cards if valid)?"

This is a statement of fact coming from the ADULT. It is not negative, in that an alternative has been suggested.

The guest, upset and coming from the CHILD, says, "My credit is good everywhere. This is a lousy place if you won't cash my check."

The cashier could respond from the CHILD by getting angry; then the two could have at it, CHILD to CHILD.

Again, a statement of fact, the ADULT speaking, "I wish I could cash the check for you without delay, and would if it were possible."

The cashier has signaled the guest to move up to the ADULT level.

The guest may be upset for failing to bring a credit card, and to turn him or her off without an attentive, responsible reply would be reprehensible.

Extra attention in times of stress may be long remembered and greatly appreciated. Guests themselves may think of alternatives.

The Disputed Charge

When checking out of a hotel, the guest recalls having

made only one phone call instead of the two being charged. "We made only one phone call and you are charging me for two! What kind of a game are you playing?"

The cashier might reply, "I'm sorry. Is it possible a friend made a call from your room?"

The cashier asks a question that moves the transaction from the CHILD to the ADULT. It could be diagrammed as below:

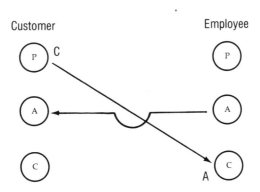

Relating to Children

Relating to children, particularly in restaurants, can be frustrating, especially when the children are tired, ill or just plain spoiled. Friendliness and firmness go hand in hand. The server, for example, must think not only of pleasing the restless child, but pleasing the other customers who may resent a noisy child, and especially one throwing a tantrum. The server can bring items such as the child's menu, a package of crackers, crayons or comic books, if available. The server must insist, however, that children not leave the table and wander around the restaurant, endangering themselves and distracting others. The service person can request that the parents or an older child to help in controlling the younger ones. Sometimes the only recourse is to ask a supervisor or a manager for help.

When Necessary, Refer to Supervisor

Demands on employees' time may preclude being able to pursue TA techniques even when TA is called for. In such cases, refer the problem to a supervisor or the manager, depending on the size of the establishment. If there is an awkward situation developing at the cashier's stand and other guests are waiting to be served, the smart decision is to refer the matter to the supervisor. To work out an awkward situation at the cashier's stand may cause more ill will among those waiting than can be gained by an immediate solution.

Employee Language and Demeanor (Greetings and Goodbyes)

As in all guest relations, choice of words and phrases helps create a pleasing environment. A server leaves an indelible guest memory when he or she says to the regular guest who is just leaving:

"I hope to see you tomorrow."

Greetings and goodbyes are, in large part, rituals, and are heard as such. A problem in guest relations is to try to avoid sounding too mechanical and to retain one's own personality. Especially to be avoided are the curt, short liners which convey a feeling of *no concern*. One of the most gauche and uncaring comments that can be made by a service employee when an apology is necessary is "Sorry about that." Apologies, when offered, must be interpreted by all concerned as absolutely genuine, and must convey tenets of the "Golden Rule" — that when you offer an apology, you place yourself in the position of the offended party and ask yourself, "How would I feel if it happened to me?" The highest compliment that could be paid to a restaurant staff would be for the guest to leave with the feeling that "The people in this place could spill coffee all over me and I'd still come back. I'd even feel sorry for the servers because I know they care."

Most guests probably would prefer not to be served by a

Pollyanna, someone excessively saccharine or overly eager to please. As mentioned earlier, a pleasant, businesslike, friendly relationship is most appreciated; one which translates into — "Welcome, we're glad you're here, and we care and are concerned about you because you are our valued guests." This is the type of demeanor in which the food or beverage server reacts to the guest's needs without being subservient or losing personal dignity.

Service personnel should not act deliberately familiar or overly solicituous. All would do well to recall the sign above the door at the Greenbriar Resort in West Virginia. "Ladies and Gentlemen being served by Ladies and Gentlemen."

Transaction Guidelines

If the guest with a problem is coming from the ADULT, he or she probably will be willing to wait a few moments for a solution while others are served. The CHILD, on the other hand, is impatient, impetuous and demanding. Immediate reference to a higher authority who has the time may be the best solution:

"With your approval, I am calling the manager, who can handle the question right away."

General Guidelines for Handling Transactions

1. As in all communication, think before you talk. Don't bore the other person by thinking out loud. Organize what you wish to say, then say it with assurance and in relatively concise terms.

2. Know what you wish to accomplish before talking. Are you trying to establish rapport? Make a person feel better? Sell someone something? Compensate for a mistake?

3. Choose your words carefully. There is nothing wrong with using carefully thought-out phrases, such as "May I be of help?" or "Would you prefer I come back later?" Avoid communications that smack of demands or of a superior talking to a subordinate. Avoid abruptness and words that may be

offensive, such as, "damn," "junk" or other slang.

4. Consider the innuendoes and overtones of what is said. Observation of the listener can tell you how your communication is being received. Is he or she acting positively, indifferently, confused, hesitating? You may be speaking too fast or too slowly. An older person may want you to speak very distinctly and very slowly. A younger person may be bored with such a pace.

5. Never suggest in any way that the guest is inferior. Disheveled guests or those in old clothes are often embarrassed. Any indication on the part of the employee that the guest is not welcome or dressed properly constitutes rudeness.

6. It is the mark of high intelligence when a person is able to communicate well with another, leaving that person feeling better about her or himself and, at the same time, accomplishing what needs to be done.

7. Probably the simplest and most direct method of uncrossing a transaction, or returning it to the ADULT level, is to ask a reasonable question, or several such questions. Questions focus attention on analysis and away from the emotional (of course, inappropriate or embarrassing questions can anger the other person, or place him or her on the defensive).

8. Another simple technique for uncrossing a transaction (or for avoiding any form of adversary position) is to change the subject.

CONCLUSION TO PART II

Presented was a simplified and condensed view of TA concepts that can be used in guest and employee relations. The purpose of PART II was to increase awareness of EGO STATES and LIFE POSITIONS of people engaged in face-to-face communications. By labeling the EGO STATES and trying to identify the feelings involved, the individual is better able to understand and improve the human relations involved. TA places the responsibility on the employee for keeping transactions on a rational level. The result should be more effective communications and better people relations.

TA attacks the age-old and constantly challenging problem of interpersonal relations. It is not a panacea, nor does its use make the user into a sensitive, wise person. It is just one more tool, another perspective, a model to use in keeping interpersonal relations rational and positive.

TA encourages sensitivity to other people's EGO STATES as well as our own, and may help to avoid unnecessary confrontations and defuse explosive situations.

Ours is a competitive society, one in which everyone is a loser at times, a society that insists the individual stand on his or her own. Our society causes us to be wary of the other person, to be on guard, to keep our defenses up so no one will take advantage. Symptoms of this include the high divorce rate, the number of people living alone, drug and alcohol abuse and the large number of people needing psychotherapy. TA in guest relations, in part, can help soften interpersonal human relations and provides, if not warmth in relations, at least good manners.

So, what is TA in guest and employee relations all about? It's about meeting guest and employee needs, both tangible and psychological, making guests a little more pleased with themselves, with the service employee and the establishment, and in helping employees take charge of these relationships with the guests, by supervisors caring for their employees.

Value is in the eye of the beholder. Guest relations adds value to the product or the service offered. Relating to guests is a continual test of one's abilities because each is somewhat different. The drama of guest relations goes on. The audience is the guest; the players are the service employees.

PART III

EMPLOYEE RELATIONS

THE BASIS OF QUALITY GUEST RELATIONS

INTRODUCTION

In Parts I and II, the basic tenets of guest relations were presented, and Transactional Analysis was proffered as a tool for improving communications. In Part III, the third ingredient will be investigated: employee relations, specifically the treatment, morale, motivation and attitudes of our employees, as controlled by how employees are managed and administered. Most employee motivation and attitudes toward guests are direct reflections of how they themselves are treated by their supervisors and junior managers. Similarly, it is how junior and middle managers are handled by their superiors up to and including top management that sets the stage for the kind of management that is passed along to the front line employee. This creates the conditions under which our guests are served. This section discusses motivational information as found in classical management theories, along with several of the identifiable management styles and their recognition by and effect on the middle and local managers and employees who serve our guests. To set the stage for understanding this important aspect of service to our guests, the following bit of history seems appropriate.

In the introduction to his book, *Marriott-The J. Willard Marriott Story,* Robert O'Brien[1] recalls the opening of the Los Angeles Airport Marriott Hotel.

For this particular Thursday in September 1973, a special excitement was in the air; special because in addition to routine business, the hotel would enjoy its "official grand opening." The hotel, having been completed several months ahead of schedule, had been operating through what was known as a 'soft opening,' and had now reached that day when it was to be officially christened, have its ribbon cut and the key to its front door officially disappear. O'Brien recalls that 13,000 people had been interviewed prior to hiring some 900 employees. And on this day, all but a skeleton group had assembled in the hotel's grand ballroom to see several members of the Marriott corporate staff issue the secret handshake to the newest members of the Marriott family.

Bud Ward, then Vice President of Organization and Development, said, "We don't have *this* Marriott and *that* Marriott; we are *all* Marriott. As you get to know our family, you're going to feel the same way." Ward said it was not just those present who were in the family, but that Marriott employees all across the country were wearing a big blue badge proclaiming "The Los Angeles Marriott Is Now Open.

Ward continued by saying, "Stick together. Work together. Have fun together." Marriott believes that the customer is great," implying also that they deserve nothing but the best, since it is the customer who pays our salaries. He concluded his comments by adding, "Mr. Marriott knows that, if he takes care of his employees, they'll take care of the customers." Ward quickly glanced at another member of the platform party who returned his glance with a smile and a wink. It was none other than the chairman himself who was soon to rise and take the floor.

A bit stooped, Bill Marriott Sr. gripped the lectern and waited for the applause to subside. In 11 days, he would be seventy-three. For 20 minutes, he talked to his employees like a father, a brother and a wise uncle. He said plain, simple and honest things, astonishing not because they were new, but because they were old, yet still valid. They were the truths he lived by.

"Well, as I've often said, anybody — almost anybody —

can't run a hotel unless they have some great people to do it." He stressed the importance of attitude, and that a college education did not mean much unless a person works hard and uses good common sense. He reflected on his mail. "People don't write and tell me how beautiful they think our hotels are; they comment on how friendly our people are. They say, 'How'd you get such friendly people?' You know, if you're interested in your job, you can do anything. I have never seen anybody who's interested in a job who couldn't do it well."

With that statement, a more subtle message began to sink in. It was as if he were saying, "I recognize your value and worth as an individual to this organization. You, I, and every other employee of this company, even though we may have different jobs to perform, are all equally important . And I will guarantee that your worth and value will be recognized, as evidenced by how supervisors and managers are going to treat you as an employee of this company."

A strange but palpable communion was in the air as he paused for a moment and looked out over his audience. He closed his presentation with several comments about overcoming problems, and the occasional dissolution we all face at times. He ended his talk with a poem dealing with the strength of character a person gains by overcoming adversity. As he stepped aside, he held up his hand in a valedictory wave and said, "I wish all of you success. I hope and pray that you will be the happiest group of people in all Los Angeles."

As he concluded, his audience, in their bright new work uniforms from every department, and the newest members of the Marriott family, applauded and cheered until the chairman departed the room.

This author, who was a member of that audience, remembers until this day, the significance of the chairman's comments, and was able to see firsthand on several following occasions the implications of his message. It seemed that no matter how menial or insignificant your job might appear to be, you were always just as valuable as anyone else in the organization. One room attendant, when asked how she could be so cheerful about having to clean 20 guest rooms every day, was heard to exclaim, "Listen, what I do at this hotel is important; and when I go home each night, I do it with a quiet heart, knowing that I have left 20 of the cleanest rooms in town for the most important people in my life — the ones who pay my salary — my guests. I like my job because what I do is important. That makes me important and my supervisor and my manager treat me with respect and confidence, and like I am somebody. They even ask me my opinions about how to make things better around here. Mr. Marriott asks me, too, when he comes to town."

CHAPTER 10

MOTIVATION

The Effect of Employee Attitudes on Guest Relations

Classical Theory

Assume a service industry job or task wherein ten employees are either involved in some form of guest contact work, or are somehow behind the scenes in a similar capacity. To do this task, the ten employees must be motivated. They are all not necessarily spirited by the same motivator, however, and the quality of the motivator may affect the manner in which the employee performs a task related to the guest.

The need for money as a motivator comes into play in a variety of ways. Some will need money primarily for survival. Others might need money to send children to school, or to go to school themselves.

Still others might perform the task as a relief from the boredom of staying at home, while others are motivated through dreams of growth in the industry. Then there are those who gravitate to an involvement with people, as opposed to the solitary position of night security officer at some factory. Suffice it to say, many people will do an identical job for a variety of different reasons, all of which are considered to be motivators.

Each motivator can cause a slightly different reaction when the employee is attempting to solve guests' problems.

Some motivators will not sustain the employee to perform in a courteous and concerned way when the attitude of the guest is less than desirable.

The manager may be overheard to say, "I motivate my people to be courteous," or to the employees he or she might say, "I am going to motivate you to be courteous to our guests." Such an approach requires the manager to assume some form of carrot-and-stick role when, in fact, the employee is being absolved from any responsibility in the matter of his or her own personal motivation. In such cases, motivators are rewards or punishments to be doled out by managers as needs arise. These managers fail to understand that motivation is a complex reaction between an individual and his or her own personal environment.[2]

Although managers and supervisors should assist in motivational development, they should do so by creating atmospheres wherein employees can motivate themselves. Techniques that imply "I am going to motivate you" are, therefore, highly suspect. To the contrary, management's sensitivity to the needs of employees culminates with an accurate understanding of what motivates certain individuals to take a desired action.

The best motivation is, therefore, self-motivation, which must come from within. Management involvement should be limited to solutions which lie in those activities over which the supervisor does have control: open communication, fair treatment, caring, sensitivity to personal needs and ensuring that employees understand their personal worth to the overall operation. Positive actions in such areas help create an environment that generates a self-motivating atmosphere.

Finally, it is rare, if not impossible, to find an employee who enjoys working for a company that has a bad reputation, is failing or has, in fact, failed. Conversely, employees enjoy and even boast about working for successful companies. In such cases, a deserved reminder that the company is successful *because* of its employees is another way of creating that positive atmosphere wherein the employee can become self-motivated to even higher levels of performance. In the hospitality industry, such employees can do well at guest problem solving. They recognize who is paying their salaries and have a genuine concern for their guests. They also see problems not as problems, but as opportunities for solutions.

Company Objectives: a Factor in Employee Motivation

Ask any hotel, restaurant or hospitality facility operator what his or her stated (in writing) company objective is, and the answers given may be startling. "To make a profit" seems to be the most readily available answer, especially to those hotel managers who don't know if their company has a *written* stated objective. Close scrutiny of some operations might cause an objective observer to exclaim, "At whose expense? The guest whose guaranteed reservation will not be honored because a personal friend of the general manager arrived unexpectedly and was given the last room? Or will it be at the expense of an ill employee who is commanded to work a double shift or run the risk of losing his or her job?" Although all hotels, restaurants or hospitality entities appear to have the same objectives - providing rooms, food, beverage and other services at a profit - there is too much room for flexibility when the phrases *quality service to the guest* and *with due regard for the employee who provides that service* are somehow omitted. It is difficult to imagine an employee wanting to be a part of a company whose stated objective is to cheat the guest and trample its employees. Yet there are some operations whose service to guests and treatment of employees come close to these guidelines.

Every service organization should take the time to specify in writing what its company objectives are. Such objectives should make reference to the conditions under which employees will be required to work and be expected to perform. This will allow prospective employees to choose (before handling guest relations problems) whether they truly desire to become a part of such organization.

Interviews: an Opportunity to Affect Motivation

During employment interviews, applicants should be made acutely aware of the importance of the part he or she is to play in the operation. This should be done in such a way that applicants can see for themselves how their contribution will help sustain the overall company objectives. Failure to do so might, at some time in the future, cause the employee to assume a feeling of worthlessness, when, in fact, such time could be put to better use in creative endeavors. Employees who sense their value and understand their contribution to a successful endeavor are more inclined to become creative when otherwise menial tasks are the only ones at hand.

Applicants should also be reminded that promotion and growth in the service industries is more a matter of likability and willingness to work hard than raw intellect. Employees that are likable, willing to work hard, creative, loyal and honest, and who will genuinely care for the guest are much more likely to grow in the industry than the person who carries only a diploma in hand.

DELEGATION: ITS EFFECT ON MOTIVATION

Learning to Trust - Then Letting Go

MCI founder Bill McGowan[3] said:

> I'm naturally a delegator. I guess I realized early in life that, unless you're going to be a violinist or something, your success was probably going to depend on other people — that's certainly true in business. And if you're going to be in a business of any size, you're going to have to develop the kind of leadership qualities that allow you to attract good people. Guide them, encourage them and ultimately trust them — and let them go and do their jobs. Oh, sure, you have to take deep breaths occasionally. But mostly you have to trust them.

Delegation is the most valuable activity within the management function of "DIRECTION". When managers delegate a task to a subordinate, they are saying, "I need you, I can't do it all myself, and I am depending on you. Here is the wherewithal, and (through training) my knowledge. You are accountable only to me for completion of the task. I will take the credit, good or bad. If you need further guidance, you must ask; but I doubt that my judgment would be any better than yours. I have confidence and trust in you to see your task and to take the proper action. If well done, your reward will be professional growth and greater responsibility in the future. Do not fear making mistakes. If you fail, your reward will be another chance."

This is a simple statement, applicable whether being said to a hotel manager about to be assigned control of a new hotel by the owners, or to a utility person who must clean the kitchen floor at 3:00 AM. In both cases, each is assigned a task, passed the power to act and held accountable for the results.

The motivational power of such action is immense because an atmosphere of trust and confidence is being established. The greatest attitude generator of all times is *to be needed.*

Why, then, do so many managers shy away from delegation? Here are a collection of reasons:[4]

1. Some managers do not understand their roles as managers. When newly promoted, they fail to see their continuous role as one who analyzes problems, makes decisions and communicates through direction and delegation. They continue to see themselves as doers, worker bees, afraid to let go, thinking that *no one* can do the job as well as they can themselves. Some managers actually enjoy the work so much they sometimes wind up with an audience — workers watching their jobs being done by their managers. It is, therefore, no surprise to find that companies promote managers who have made themselves dispensable (not indispensable) in a current job.

2. Less-competent people fear the consequences of being outperformed. Some managers refuse to delegate routine tasks for fear their own incompetence will be magnified. Their incompetence is in management, not in doing that which they refuse to delegate.

3. Some managers feel that delegation is an all-or-nothing situation. There are degrees of delegation, and the manager must separate all sundry tasks that must be done into three groups: one group of tasks that any subordinate can do now, if assigned; a second group that requires specific training prior to delegation; and the third group that can only be done by the manager. The largest group of tasks is always found in group one. The manager's group three is the smallest. But the first task in group three is to train employees to do the tasks in group two. Employee relations are greatly enhanced in those organizations where delegation is widespread and no manager is indispensable.

The Most Forceful Motivator - Examples Set by Those Above

If service employees are to provide continuous quality, courtesy and concerned service to all who become our valued guests and patrons, it is because of a self-motivating force within the employee to be a part of something worthwhile.

Additionally, most employees, if given a chance, will choose to recognize the Golden Rule as a guide to functioning in daily operations. If workers are to set the right kind of courteous and concerned example to the guests, the example must extend from top management through the middle managers and supervisors to the employee.

Example, then, must extend from top management down to include all layers of personnel within the organization. Also, it is crucial that management and supervision at all levels understand, acknowledge and believe in the company objective. Each person should take every opportunity to reaffirm the value and worth of every individual to every other individual in the company.

The utility person who mops the kitchen floor at 3:00 A.M. and the general manager should be able to sit down together and have a cup of coffee, look at each other and say, "We are paid at different rates because our skills and responsibilities are different. We do different things, but what each of us does is vital to the operation. We, therefore, as individuals, are both vital and the operation cannot do without either one of us." In such an environment, everyone, including the guests, will benefit.

ENDNOTES

1. Robert O'Brien, *Marriott: The J. Willard Marriott Story* (Salt Lake City: Deseret Book Company, 1977), Chapter 1, pp.1-11.

2. Robert J. Martin, adapted from his book *Professional Management Of Housekeeping Operations* (New York: John Wiley and Sons, Inc., 1976), p. 337.

3. Bill McGowan (MCI Founder) (as reported in a feature, *Face-to-Face.* Interviewed by editors Bo Burlingame and Steven Pearlstein, INC. Magazine), August, 1986, p. 29.

4. Robert J. Martin, *op. cit.*, pp. 16-17.

CHAPTER 11

MANAGEMENT SYSTEMS

Their Recognition and Effect on Employee Relations

Evolution of Classical Styles - McGregor's X and Y Theory

The evolution of classical management theory has produced some remarkable literature, none of which is more powerful or pertinent to the way managements communicate to their members than Douglas McGregor's Theory X and Theory Y. Management's technique in communicating becomes even more evident when we investigate the several "management systems" that have been defined by other management authors. When management's communications to its workers are limited to directives, performance appraisals and disciplinary actions, and are lacking in the personal element, workers become suspicious of management, and control by fear becomes commonplace. Such environments affect morale, and the personal motivators of those serving the guest digress from esteem and self-realization to survival and security. There is, therefore, a need to understand McGregor's theories, which are restated for review.

His *Theory X* assumption is summarized in the following four statements:[1]

1. Work, if not downright distasteful, is an onerous task that must be performed in order to survive.

2. The average human being has an inherent dislike of work and will avoid it if he can.

3. Because of the human characteristic to dislike work, most people must be coerced, directed, controlled or threatened with punishment to get them to put forth adequate effort toward the achievement of organizational objectives.

4. The average human being prefers to be directed, wishes to avoid responsibility, has relatively little ambition and wants security above all else.*

Simply stated, Theory X indicates that there is no intrinsic satisfaction in work, that human beings avoid it as much as possible, that positive direction is needed to achieve organization goals and that workers possess little ambition or originality.

Theory X also assumes that most people prefer to be directed, are not interested in assuming responsibility and want security above all else. Along with this viewpoint is the belief that people are motivated by money, fringe benefits and the threat of punishment. Managers who believe in Theory X try to tightly control and closely supervise employees. They feel that external control is needed for dealing with people because people, in their eyes, are unreliable, irresponsible and immature.

McGregor, after much observation and study, concluded that Theory X assumptions about the nature of human beings are generally inaccurate and that a management approach based on this concept will fail to motivate people to work toward company goals. He pointed out that management by direction and control is a questionable method for creating environments whereby employees can become motivated. If their physiological needs have been reasonably satisfied, employees are largely concerned about their drives for affiliation, self-esteem and self-realization, he noted.

As a result, McGregor developed an alternate theory of human behavior and called it *Theory Y*. His six assumptions for Theory Y are as follows:[2].

1. The expenditure of physical and mental effort in work is as normal as effort extended in play. The average human being does not inherently dislike work. Depending upon working conditions, work may be a source of pride and will be performed voluntarily.

2. External control and the threat of punishment are not the only means for bringing about effort toward organizational objectives. People will exercise self-direction and self-control in the service of objectives to which they are committed.

3. Commitment to objectives is a function of the awards associated with their achievement. The most significant of such work, e.g., the satisfaction of ego and self-actualization needs, can be direct products of efforts directed toward organizational objectives.

4. The average human learns under proper conditions not only to accept but to seek responsibility. Avoidance of responsibility, lack of ambition and emphasis on security are general consequences of experience, not inherent human characteristics.

5. The capacity to exercise a relatively high degree of imagination, ingenuity and creativity in the solution of organization problems is widely, not narrowly, distributed in the population.

6. Under the conditions of modern industrial life, the intellectual potentials of the average human beings are only partially utilized.

This theory assumes that people are *not*, by nature, lazy and unreliable, but are basically self-directed and creative at work if properly motivated. Therefore, it becomes the essential job of management and supervisors to unleash this potential in each worker so the company and the guests will get full benefit from the worker's knowledge, experience and creativity.

The fact that there is an opposite way of thinking about workers in the above two theories is obvious. What is not so obvious, however, is the fact that a manager or supervisor can communicate what theory he or she is operating under, simply by the manner in which they say, *"Good morning."*

Four Classical Management Systems

If you strip away the semantics used to label various approaches to management, it will be noted that most American firms operate under one of the four following systems.[3]

SYSTEM 1

Management is seen by employees as having little or no confidence and trust in subordinates. Most employees are not involved in the decision-making process.

Decisions and company goals are set at the top and are passed down the chain of command.

The employee working climate is full of fear, threats, punishment and, only occasionally, rewards. The only motivation is satisfaction of basic physiological human needs. Whatever superior-subordinate interaction takes place is within a relationship marked by mutual fear and mistrust. While control over decisions and goals is highly concentrated in top management, an informal organization generally develops among subordinates which tends to oppose all of the goals of the formal organization.

SYSTEM 2

Management offers a master-servant relationship with employees. A condescending confidence and trust in subordinates exists, but the major volume of decisions are made at the top along with all company goals. Some decisions are made at lower levels, but only within a prescribed framework or control.

Rewards and some actual or potential punishments are used to motivate workers. Any superior-subordinate interaction is done with some condescension by top management, but with fear and caution by subordinates.

While the control process is still very much concentrated in top management, some is delegated to middle and lower levels of the firm. An informal organization develops below the top management level. In some instances, the informal organization may resist goals set by formal management.

SYSTEM 3

Management has substantial but not complete trust and confidence in subordinates. Broad policy and general decisions are still retained at the top, but subordinates are allowed to make more of the specific decisions at lower levels.

Communication flows both up and down the organization structure. Rewards, occasional punishment and some involvement in managing the company are used to motivate workers. There is a moderate amount of superior-subordinate interaction, much of which is done in a climate of confidence and trust. Significant tasks within the control process are delegated downward and a feeling of responsibility is shared at both higher and lower levels. The informal organization may develop, but it will often support top management goals and may only occasionally resist pressure from above.

SYSTEM 4

Management is seen as having complete confidence and trust in subordinates. Decision-making is widely spread throughout the company, but decisions are integrated for maximum effectiveness.

Communication flows not only up and down but among peers. Employees are motivated by participation and management involvement.

Employees develop their own economic rewards, set their own production goals, improve their own methods of operation and appraise their own progress toward goals.

The company has extensive, friendly superior-subordinate interaction with a high level of confidence and trust. Responsibility for the control process is widespread, with all lower units fully involved. The informal and formal organization are often one and the same. The result is that all social drives support efforts to achieve defined organizational goals.

Summarizing the Systems

In summary, System 1 is a task-oriented, highly structured, authoritarian style of management. It can be defined as *Authoritative Exploitative*, heavily laden at the top with Theory X-type people. As a result, Theory X thinking eventually permeates the entire supervisory structure as it becomes known as, "the only way to get ahead."

Systems 2 and 3 are intermediate stages between the two extremes. Certain characteristics will come close to the assumptions in McGregor's X or Y. System 2 can be labeled *Authoritative Benevolent* (or the benevolent dictatorship) and System 3 is known as *Consultative.*

System 4 is a relationships-oriented management system based on mutual trust, non-threatening teamwork and confidence. It can be properly labeled as the *Participative* style of management and is equated to McGregor's Theory 'Y' assumptions about people and how they communicate with each other throughout the organization.

Forces In Combination

Management systems conjure the thought of "style," and style is another way of viewing communications that take place within a given management framework. In reviewing management systems, it is important to imagine the kind of communications that are prevalent within that functioning system. The reader should also imagine the effect that a certain manner of communicating would have on the atmosphere in which a guest-contact employee is required to operate. Superimpose also the aspects of TA; then imagine all such forces at work simultaneously. The guest-contact employee may be in for some rough terrain.

For example: Consider the employee who works for a company that communicates a strong Theory X tendency, and who is having to relate to a guest with a strong CRITICAL PARENT or REBEL CHILD attitude. This employee might quickly inform his or her supervisor what can be done with his job; or, worse yet, might not show up for work tomorrow. In these situations, management always seems surprised and usually never finds out why the employee deserted his or her job.

System 4 - A Requirement for Trust and Confidence

System 4 provides for work to be as natural as play and equally enjoyable. Also, that a person's own self-control and self-discipline are vital if they are to help achieve organizational goals. The potential for creativity in solving company and guest relations problems is widely distributed in the population and will surface if given the right working environment.

Managers who have the Theory Y viewpoint do not usually attempt to structure, control or closely supervise the work environment. Instead, they try to help their employees mature by exposing them to progressively less external control, allowing them to assume more and more self-control. Employees working in this type of environment are able to achieve the satisfaction of esteem, affiliation and self-realization.

In the participative style of management, McGregor's Theory Y is fully activated. Lower operating cost, higher morale, low turnover, low absenteeism, greater overall efficiency, a smoother running operation and less theft are augmented by having a group of employees who see their objectives as parallel to company objectives. In other words, in the hospitality industry, we find employees who are positively challenged by quality and concerned service to the guest, and by guest problem solving. The employee's challenge is to become less adversarial in relationships with the company and more recognizing of the most important person in the establishment - the guest.

Situation Management

The implication above is that System 4 (participative management) rings through as the panacea for all employee relations problems. This type of thinking implies that all applicants seeking employment are waiting to have their self-esteem coddled and their self-actualization tantalized. To the contrary, too many people seeking employment in the hospitality field are searching for survival, trying to satisfy their physiological and security needs. A transient employee, searching for a day's subsistence, is not necessarily turned on by how well he or she can solve a problem for the affluent guest. And such person usually has little confidence that the same job will be waiting for them tomorrow.

Management may be required to attune more to a specific "situation" than to an academic philosophy.

Conclusion

Management must assess situations and be selective as to who is best qualified to handle certain assignments. It is, therefore, *enlightened delegation* that becomes the challenge: who to delegate to, what to delegate and what will be the degree of control and accountability needed based on a given situation. Management must recognize that each worker is driven by a different set of motivators, and must learn what is motivating each individual. Management must then create the atmosphere in which that motivator can flourish for each employee. This is best done by learning good communication techniques which identify the communicator as primarily a

Theory Y manager, with the capability of responding in Theory X fashion if the building catches fire.

Employee relations affect guest relations. Employee relations may be affected even by company objectives. It therefore behooves every manager to understand and apply good management and communication skills in securing the best of employee relations from the top to the bottom in the organization.

In APPENDIX C there is a leadership questionnaire which tends to indicate a person's supervisory or management style. The reader is encouraged to examine his or her own styles for reference information.

ENDNOTES

1. Douglas McGregor, *The Human Side Of Enterprise* (New York: McGraw Hill Book Co.,1960), pp. viii, 33-34, 246.

*. Assumptions 2, 3, and 4 are quoted directly from McGregor (Ref. 3). Assumption 1 has been added as an explicit statement of the nature of the work to which humans are reacting.

2. Douglas McGregor, *op. cit.* pp. 47-48.

3. Rensis Likert, *New Patterns of Management* (New York: McGraw Hill, 1961), Chapt. 14, pp. 224-236.

CHAPTER 12

GROUP DYNAMICS

Group Consensus and the Managerial Grid

Introduction

Contrary to what many people believe, there is nothing inherently good or bad about groups and group action. Groups (and this term is meant to include all human assemblies from committees and social clubs to project teams and departments) have certain unique properties, it is true; but from a performance standpoint, groups function as their members make them function.

Assume that a group of six people are working on a problem. It may be presumed that each individual is in possession of some of the information needed to make a quality decision, but not all of it. It then becomes a task of the group to bring forth all the information that the group as a whole embraces. If this does occur, the group is known to be synergistic, and the group answer to the problem should be a better answer than the answer held by any one of the individual group members.

As the characteristics of specific groups are explored, both potentials and pitfalls are discovered. There are those members who "carry the conversation" and the crowd, to the exclusion of others - and not necessarily to the best decision. And to the contrary, there are those whose information provides a better solution, but the individual group member is unable to convince the group. Then there are those who sit quietly and do not participate.

The hospitality industry requires heavy group participation due to the administration of large staffs. Also, there are many meetings involving scheduling, budgeting, informing employees about events to come and establishing operating procedures and general policy. Many such groups become involved in decision making and policy development.

Group activity can have a direct effect on the morale environment and, as result, an effect on employee relations. For this reason, a study of group activity and dynamics is most important.

Group Decision Process - Reaching a Consensus

Research in group dynamics has revealed that the manner in which groups utilize their member resources is a critical determinant of how they perform. Some groups may have as their objective arriving at a CONSENSUS. Reaching a consensus is not always easy; it is not taking a majority vote. Neither is unanimity a goal (although it can be achieved unintentionally).

It is not necessary that every person be completely satisfied as if he or she had complete control over the total group. What must be stressed is the individual's ability to accept a given decision on the basis of logic, regardless of satisfaction level, and a willingness to entertain a judgment as feasible. When all members reach this point as a minimum criterion, a consensus can often be reached.

Here are some general guidelines for achieving consensus:

1. Avoid arguing for your point. Present your position as logically as possible. But consider the reactions of the group to other presentations on the same point.

2. Don't try to force win-lose situations. Good consensus does not require that there be a winner and loser. If an impasse occurs, look for the next best alternative suitable to both sides of the point.

3. Do not change your mind only in order to avoid conflict and reach agreement in harmony. Pressures to give in which have no logical basis in fact should be resisted. Strive for enlightened flexibility; avoid outright capitulation.

4. Avoid reducing techniques such as majority vote, averaging, bargaining, coin-flipping and other similar contrivances.

5. View differences in opinion as helpful and natural. The more opinions expressed, the greater the likelihood for conflict; but the richer the possibilities will be for quality decisions.

6. View initial agreements as suspect. Explore the underlying reasons for apparent agreements. Make sure people have arrived at similar conclusions based on the same or complementary logic.

7. Avoid subtle forms of influence and decision modification. Do not buy the dissenting member's agreement with any form of reward.

8. Consider the possibility that your group can excel; avoid negativism.

There will be many times that employees at all levels of the organization will have an opportunity to participate in group activity in which decisions are the objective. Seldom do employees enjoy participating in group activity, however, when they feel at a disadvantage because of their lack of experience, formal education or position in the organization. Group activity such as working for a consensus should be a part of training programs in group dynamics. This is another technique wherein employee relations may be strengthened.

Breakthrough In Organizational Development

Having highlighted the need to understand the importance of individual employee relationships and how they may affect guest relations, there is yet another trend in employee development that warrants investigation.

Henry L. Sisk[1] reminds us that many managers have commented from time to time upon the importance of "an organizational climate," indicating how its negative effect on the application of skills and attitudes acquired during training may occur.

Considerable expenditure is made in training employees how to respond or react to guest concerns, and how to apply problem-solving techniques, only to find such skills erode away with the passing of time.

High-performing employees are often rewarded with promotion, only to be neglected in supervisory or junior management training in their new found skills. A particular area where training is neglected is in the subject of group dynamics.

What might happen to the quality of guest relations if it were possible to alter the organizational climate in which the guest-contact employees find themselves?

Organizational Climate

It has been argued that organizational climate is the result of the manner in which all policies are executed - not the result of a specific decision. What effect, then, can a determined leadership have over its style of management and, as a result, effect a major change in its organizational climate? What if all supervisory members of the organization were to participate in a program designed to change attitudes toward oneself and toward others? Since the point has been made for "participative management," what would happen if we were to achieve *organizational development* as well as training in human relations skills?

A Landmark Case in Organization Development

Companies engaged in hospitality operations have in recent years become keenly interested in a study which became a major breakthrough in *organization development*[2].

All 800 management members of a Texas production company known as Sigma, participated in a "management grid" training program. Four members of the company's top management were involved first. Then training was given by top management to its subordinates, and so on until all members of the company supervisory structure had been involved.

Results of the study included an improvement of profit by 55 percent, a 69 percent reduction in operating costs and a 35 percent improvement in productivity. Of those participating in the grid training experiment, only 16 percent rated the program as somewhat low, while 84 percent rated the program highly or very highly.

There was also a subsequent increase in the number of meetings held with employees, indicating an increased group effort in problem solving.

It was also learned that, for an organization development program to be a success, the application of what we know concerning leadership, communications and motivation, top management need not only give its enthusiastic support to such training, it must also become the program's internal administrator.

What was learned in the Sigma studies has been shown to have great merit in the training and administration of hospitality workers, from top management through and including all levels of employees working in a "participative" atmosphere.

(The author participated in a management grid seminar in Washington D.C. in 1975, while an employee of the Marriott Corporation, and found it to be the most rewarding professional development experience of his career. Based on personal experi-

ences, and on the finding of the Sigma studies, practice and understanding of the management grid and its relationship to human dynamics for the hospitality industry is highly recommended. The basic tenets of the management grid system follow.)

The Management Grid

Whereas *sensitivity training* usually engages the individual in an introspective analysis of her or himself, the management grid[3] directs attention toward managerial styles. Grid training is usually broken down into two major phases. The first phase is devoted to teaching the grid system, and the second phase involves team and intergroup development, goal setting and goal attainment. For simplicity, only the system itself will be presented here.

A Concern for Production

Recall the classical definition of management simply stated as "getting things done through people." What happens, however, when other managers having the same responsibility are in conflict with us as to the *best way* to achieve getting things done? How do we influence others to see our point of view, or how do others persuade us to change our minds?

Better yet, how do we find solutions to problems in such a way as to get the commitment and involvement of our peers and our subordinates?

In the hospitality world, production may be thought of as problem solving, making decisions that others will implement, making policy that affects all aspects of hotel operations, including guest relations, or resolving problems in department operations which impinge on other departments. Having a concern for the accomplishment of such work in these areas might therefore be considered as *a concern for production*. Most such decisions cannot be made in a vacuum. They require the input and concern of all for the effect such decisions may have on others in the organization, and on their own areas of concern.

A Concern for People

Since managers do not necessarily do work, but manage the people who do, another concern that must be addressed is how to relate to people, and how to relate people to the production effort. A *concern for people,* then, becomes an equally compelling issue.

Since both concerns must be present to a greater or lesser degree when we are thinking in a management way, the grid relates each of these two concerns to each other in a measurable form. The grid system further directs attention to several management styles that may be charted.

The grid (Figure 2), has a vertical axis which relates to *a concern for production* and a horizontal axis which relates to *a concern for people.*

Note the vertical axis indicating *a concern for production* with a minimum value of 1 to a maximum value of 9, and the horizontal axis indicating *a concern for people,* also having a minimum value of 1 and maximum value of 9.

Superimposed on the grid are five management styles relating to a minimum or maximum concern for people or production. Sisk identifies these styles as follows:[4]

1.1. A minimum effort to get work done but sufficient to maintain organization.

9.1. Emphasis on work with minimum interference from human factors.

1.9. Primary attention to the needs of people; a comfortable place to work.

5.5. Balance between attention to work and attention to people.

9.9. Work is accomplished by people committed to the organization; a high degree of congruence between the goals of the organization and goals of individuals.

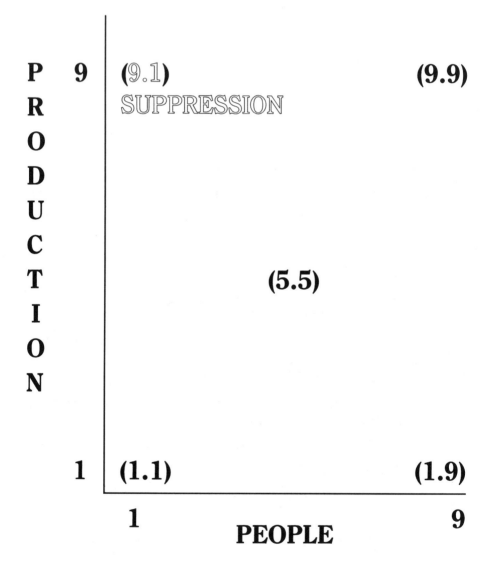

RESOLUTION OF CONFLICT

FIGURE 2

The grid implies that an unlimited number of management styles may result from varying combinations of concern for production or people. The grid advocate, however, generalizes five separate and distinct styles that may be categorized.

An organization can be identified as having any one of the five management styles, depending on how the organization is viewed by others.

However, it is more appropriate to imagine each member of the management group as having a particular individual style, and interacting with other members of the group having similar or, more likely, different individual styles. Imagine the effect on the quality of production decisions on the one hand, and a possible effect on employee morale, loyalty and commitment on the other hand.

Resolution of Conflict

Imagine a group of decision makers getting together to decide on several policies. If each member of the group has essentially the same point of view, regardless of management style, a decision comes easily and the group moves on to other matters. Imagine, however, that on the next issue one or more of the group members has a differing point of view, and a different management style. Conflict is certain to arise.

Conflict: Two or more people have differing points of view. A disagreement is present that must be resolved before decisions can be made. In the course of finding a solution, feelings arise, and emotions come into the thoughts and minds of decision-makers.

The problem is that conflict has a major side effect — *frustration*. And frustration has its own set of rules.

1. Frustration plus *dependence* yields *hate.*

2. Frustration plus a desire to *destroy the source* yields *murder.*

3. Since murder is not recognized as an acceptable method of coping, we find more mundane ways of dealing with

frustration.

4. We may — Withdraw from the scene of battle.

— Stay in and fight back underhandedly.

— Join forces and beat down the opposition.

— Attempt to smooth over the disagreement.

— Compromise.

— Defer the decision and search for better facts.

— Set the main problem aside temporarily and investigate the nature of the conflict itself.

When a group is in conflict, it is most often the *method of conflict resolution used* which helps us clearly define the management styles in evidence. What follows is an in-depth explanation of each management style and its associated methods of conflict resolution.

THE GRID STYLE POSITIONS

All styles are identified by recognizing "a person's way of thinking about problem solving."

The 9.1 Style

The 9.1 style is, therefore, thought of as a very well-known way of thinking about solutions to problems. This type of thinker has a high regard for getting things done, work accomplished and decisions made that stick. There will be little concern, however, for the people who may be involved in the decision or its aftermath. The 9.1 thinker somehow believes that there is an inevitable contradiction between the organizational needs of production and the personal needs of people. One thought monopolizes this thinker's concern and action, and that is production. The 9.1 thinker personifies the entrepreneurial spirit. Usually in a position of authority, and sensing it, this person sees his or her responsibilities as only to PLAN, DIRECT and CONTROL in whatever way necessary to get the job done. Schedules are to be met. People are expected to do what they are told; no more - no less. The 9.1 style has been described in many other ways:

Autocratic vs. Democratic

Production vs. People Oriented

Authoritarian vs. Participative

Scientific vs. Human Relations Oriented

Theory X vs. Theory Y.

9.1 is not a very hard way to think. All the manager thinks he or she must do is state a policy or requirement. Any disagreement can usually be disregarded.

"Look, don't tell me why you can't do it; show me how you can." It may not provide the best decision, but it is efficient. And if the employee can't do the job, he or she can be replaced. 9.1 is not a very complex way of thinking.

How then is the 9.1 thinker resolving conflict? *By suppression.* "I'm the boss, you do what I say. You have one point of view, I have another. I try to get you to see the wisdom of my point, but you still resist, and, if I am thinking in a 9.1 way, I don't much like your resistance. As a matter of fact, it makes me a little annoyed. So do it before I get really annoyed!"

You agree because of your subordinate position; you really have no other choice. Action can now be taken; the conflict is gone.

Ironically, the 9.1 thinker is not pained by conflict. It is an everyday part of his or her life. Such a person is used to it, not bothered by it, is hardened to it and always manages it the same way: by suppression.

If two 9.1 thinkers become involved in the same conflict, the arena of battle becomes much more intense. Each attempts to outdo and outmaneuver the other until eventually there is a winner. When this happens, the loser, in frustration, may attempt to *fight back underhandedly* on a future occasion.

To get back at the other person, but to do it so as not to get caught, takes great creative thinking. Possibly to withhold information that can cause another person to stumble and fall. Sabotage the person, then aid him or her in seeing the depths of their error. This is commonly known as infighting.

Or the loser could bring about a *joining of forces* against the victor in some future setting.

Should the above scenarios describe a pattern which continues over a long period of time, the loser may eventually *withdraw from the scene of battle* and take on a different management style (usually 1.1, with a new attitude of "who cares").

The 9.1 style of thinking about management decisions is not very hard to accomplish, nor is the technique hard to acquire. It is, however, one way of thinking about how to remove conflict — *with a high degree of concern for production and a minimum concern for people*. In Figure 3, the management grid shown in Figure 2 is augmented to show the technique of conflict resolution used by the 9.1.thinker.

The 1.9 Style

The 1.9 is quite a different way of thinking and of managing. Sometimes known as "country club management," it supports the *modern milk* theory of production, i.e., people, like contented cows, should produce good milk. This has never been proven, but it sounds good. Unfortunately, many things — including *the store* — have been given away in the name of achieving production without actually having any real effect on production.

The scenario of the 1.9 thinker is much like the following when relating to subordinates:

"I would like no disagreements because they make me very anxious. I feel very uncomfortable when people are disagreeing with me." The 1.9 thinker is an overly sensitive person who surmises, "I'm not sure if I'm being accepted when I become embroiled in disagreement. The best thing I

RESOLUTION OF CONFLICT

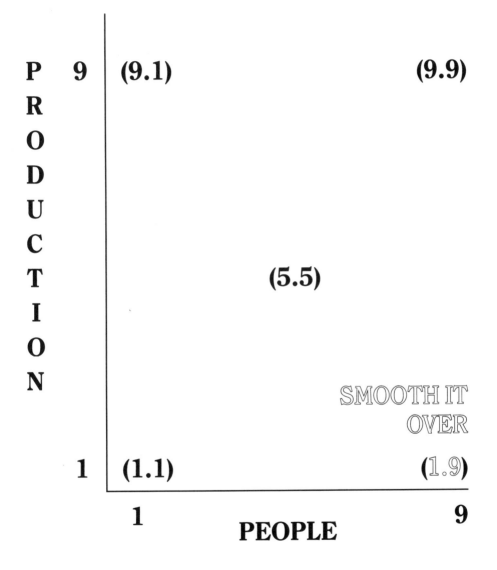

FIGURE 3

can do is act toward you in such a way that you will like me, and I really know how to do that."

The 1.9 thinker tries to avoid putting anything on workers that might cause them to strain or toil. By not generating a situation between themselves and their workers, the hope is that in some way, each person will see his or her own responsibilities and carry them out. And "When you and I see each other, we can talk about our vacations, families, hobbies, children and your health; things which are not a source of tension between us. You can like me because I am not forcing my demands on you, and in this way, we can get along very well." Production may go down the drain, but at least we have a happy workplace.

Many times, situations can be managed in just such a way, but this does not address the quality of the decisions made which, in the long, run will affect both the worker and the organization.

Pressures from above create quite a different and more severe problem for the 1.9 thinker. The goal — to be liked — is now in real jeopardy.

The 1.9 thinker concludes, "If I must make a choice, I have to be liked by my boss more than by my subordinates, since he or she is the source of my ultimate security. When I have a production problem that I must confront my employees with, I'll do it, but in such a way as to nourish the affection of my workers."

The 1.9 thinker *smoothes it over* and tries to make the problem seem unimportant. The following cliches are always there for the 1.9 thinker to fall back on in hopes that the employees won't take the "setback" of having to work, in a negative way.

"This is just a momentary situation. The sun will shine tomorrow."

"We must all practice the art of positive thinking."

"Let's remember how good we've had it all these years. Count our blessings."

"We have to take a little of the vinegar with the greens, a little of the bitter with the sweet."

The 1.9 thinker then concludes by saying, "Our long and friendly relationship can continue to flourish, and we won't have to be irritated by the disagreeable little bits of work we all have to do now and then."

Some 1.9 managers feel that relationships generated in one setting, transfer into another. The manager who sets the stage for friendly relationships in a social setting and assumes that these genteel feelings will transfer into a professional setting is most times disappointed. "If we play together well, we should work together well, so let's all go on a fishing trip and get to know each other better." This technique in group dynamics is quite questionable.

Finally, after the 1.9 manager's years of taking heat from the boss that the manager chose not to pass down to the employees, the manager is devastated when the employees turn on him and attempt to unionize. As a comparison, in quick summary:

The 9.1 manager "suppresses" conflict by putting others under his or her thumb, feeling no ill as a result.

The 1.9 manager tries to *smooth over* conflict, sensing the onslaught of a case of ulcers.

The 1.9 method of conflict resolution is depicted in Figure 3.

The 5.5 Style

The 5.5 thinker employs the following line of thought:

"I know I ought to push for production but I'd better not go all out and gain the reputation of being a hard-nose. That type doesn't usually get along with our company philosophy very well. Therefore, I'd better

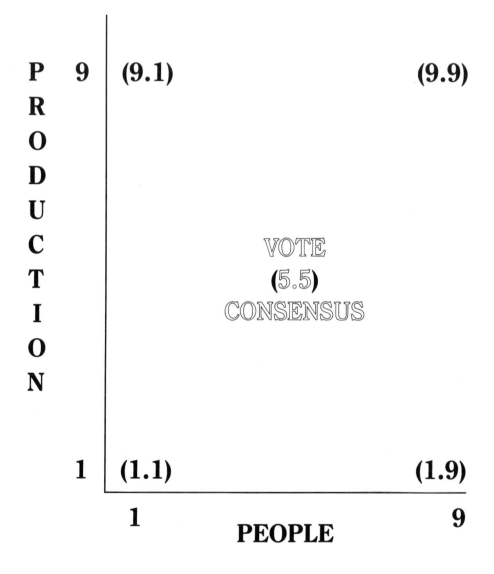

FIGURE 4

show my interest in people, because morale and the attitudes of others are important in this company. However, I'd better not go all out for people and get a reputation for being soft. I'll split the difference and *COMPROMISE*."

The solution to the avoidance of conflict for the 5.5 thinker is: "Stick close to tradition, precedents and past practices. After all, who would criticize this type of behavior? Leave innovation to others. They're usually wrong anyway. After the new idea has been proven, then I'll embrace it - if it works."

If conflict does arise, attempt to reach a consensus - promote some middle ground for compromise. If that will not work, "Vote!"

Splitting the difference through compromise seems to be a very widespread way of obtaining agreement. Also, compromise is an instrument of political action. There is no attempt to explore why people feel the way they do. Just, "Come on, folks, let's accept the consensus point of view and move on to the next problem." What usually happens? If the project fails, you hear, "See, I told you it wouldn't work." An idea may not work because, when tough decisions had to be made, there was no attempt to work through complex situations.

Another 5.5 tactic: sound out the feelings of the group members *before* decision time. Then at the meeting, the 5.5 manager is in a position to side with the majority - not because it is right, but because it is popular.

This is what is known as *"antenna management."* The soundness of the decision may suffer, but at least several others made a bad decision, too. In this case, the 5.5 manager has avoided being out on a limb alone.

Figure 4 adds the 5.5 method of conflict resolution to the management grid.

The 1.1. Style

Drs. Blake and Mouton could show that the 9.1, 1.9 and 5.5

RESOLUTION OF CONFLICT

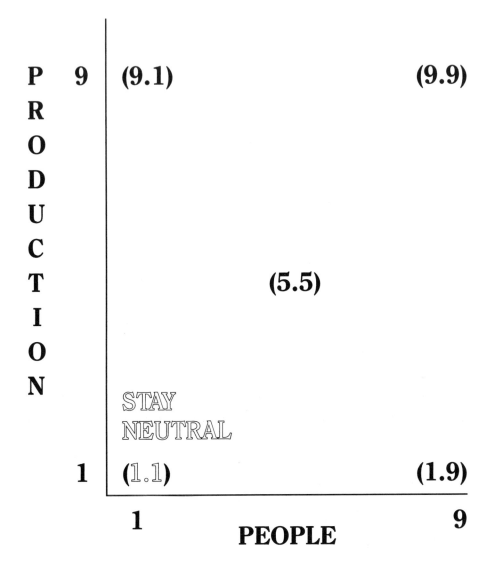

FIGURE 5

managers were obvious in the management setting. It took a little time, however, to accept the fact that a person could actually think in a 1.1. way and still survive in today's management arena. It is true, however, that some managers do think in a 1.1. way, and the examples are more prevalent than we might care to think.

The presence of the 1.1 thinker is most often recognized by such thinker having a neutral stance when conflict is present. By staying neutral and having the "skill" to resist expressing an opinion, there is a chance that the 1.1 manager won't even be noticed, because the talkative loudmouths seem to find each other, enjoy their antagonisms and have little time to observe the quiet bystander. The 1.1 thinker continues then to stay out of and make no contribution to resolving the problem or the conflict. The scenario becomes, "If you don't offer an opinion, you can't be quoted. As a result, you can't be held accountable." This becomes a much easier way of attaining retirement than to transfer energy, emotions and feelings into involvement and worry.

Researchers have now uncovered the perfect 1.1 profile. The manager is vivacious off the job, highly programmed on the job in a very mechanical way, and usually a little above a middle manager. This manager is always on time, never late, therefore never noticeable by absence. This 1.1 thinker goes to meetings with a clipboard and takes copious and careful notes. Due to the politeness of others, a person taking notes is seldom interrupted and asked for an opinion. And most certainly, a person cannot be criticized for taking notes, going back and communicating "unedited" instruction to others; yet the 1.1 thinker is *never involved*. Since the 1.1 thinker is never interrupted to be asked for an opinion, others in the group go on to find solutions among themselves. This manager is never trapped. In relating to his or her own employees, the 1.1 thinker practices a form of "reverse documentation." Records are kept of meetings with subordinates which, if necessary, could assure his or her superiors that "I passed the word" which had been discussed at the earlier meeting when those notes were taken.

This, then, becomes the strategy: be present, on time, act involved. Seem interested, but do nothing that smacks of controversy or is subject to criticism, and inwardly hold the feeling, "I couldn't care less."

Consider this three-level meeting as an example: You, your subordinate and your supervisor are present. Your boss asks your opinion on a matter. You say, " Oh, I wouldn't want to influence anyone at this point." Turning to your subordinate, you say, "What do you think?"

Failing to contribute anything of value to group discussions, most 1.1 thinkers in business get kicked upstairs, since there is a need to get them out of the way and make room for those who will make meaningful contributions to production decisions; even all the way to retirement (ideally, early retirement).

The 1.1 thinker's method of resolving conflict, then, is by *staying neutral.* Figure 5 summarizes this point by noting the grid 1.1 style method for conflict resolution.

The 9.9 Style

Whereas the four previous styles occur naturally in the management setting, 9.9 is a synthetic style that must be developed and constantly practiced if the technique is to be learned, or else one will slip back into the other *natural styles.*

To have the highest degree of concern for production while holding the highest degree of concern for people is at first considered by some as a pipe dream. To understand the 9.9 style is to understand the dynamics of *commitment* and *involvement.*

Commitment is the act of pledging oneself to the principles and goals or activities of a particular organizational unit, and then to the total enterprise. Commitment implies more than agreement or passive acceptance of an idea, project or person. It implies a willingness to support and actively work toward

RESOLVING CONFLICT IN 9.9

1. <u>Dig for better facts!</u>

- ☐ MORE COMPELLING
- ☐ NEUTRAL
- ☐ HAVE STERILE QUALITY

2. <u>Investigate the conflict itself.</u>

FIGURE 6

fulfillment of a meaningful goal.

Involvement is a similar but stronger term for the same phenomenon. Ego involvement of self relates back to what has been mentioned in other chapters — the need to be a part of something worthwhile. The employee must have the vision and understanding to say, "The goals of the organization are my goals. In fulfilling company goals, my own personal goals will also be satisfied. Whatever I have to offer becomes an integral part of the success of the organization to which I belong, and as a result, if the company prospers, I will prosper as an individual."

Again, the primary difference between 9.9 and all other management styles is found in the techniques employed to resolve conflict. The 9.9 thinker uses two basic techniques:

1. By presentation of better, more objective, neutral (and thereby more compelling) facts.

2. By confrontation of the conflict itself (to explore why people are thinking the way they do). The job is to literally break down the facades and barriers to actions that are truly worth committing oneself.

The first technique includes the two following steps:

1. Dig for better, more compelling or objective facts. Facts have a highly neutral and sterile quality, and great intellectual appeal that can bring about the changing of minds. There is nothing wrong with the changing of one's mind. This is not being wishy-washy, neutral or yielding, but responding to the creation of a position that was not available before new facts were produced.

2. Test, experiment, explore, challenge. New results can resolve disagreements (conflicts) as to a better course of action.

When the disagreement is not subject to resolution, either because facts are not available or because the problem is not in the factual area, then the second technique must be brought into play. The conflict itself must be confronted head-on. The following steps are important:

1. Before trying to solve the primary problem, it must be temporarily set aside, and the conflict itself must be confronted.

2. The emotions that underlie the disagreement must be revealed, studied and dealt with.

3. The group must attempt to learn why other group members are digging in their heels, are so unyielding and reacting in an emotional way. It is not always a pleasant experience when you must have your armor pierced — the armor we often carry around as protection, better known as our facade. Yet the causes of many disagreements are based on our personal values and prejudices. It takes great skill to arrest the disagreement over a main problem long enough to make a penetrating examination of group relations and conditions of emotional disagreement. There is usually no other way to get rid of the problems that exist in *relationships*, other than to confront the relationships head-on.

Figure 6 identifies the methods of conflict resolution for the 9.9 style.

A Review of Conflict Resolution for Each Management Style

Recalling that it is the manner in which each style resolves conflict that helps identify the style, let us look at a short review:

For 9.1, "It's going to be this way because I said so." Conflict is suppressed. There is no personal remorse.

For 1.9, "To get along, you have to go along." Conflict is smoothed over. This manager gets ulcers.

For 5.5, "Let's vote. Maybe we have a consensus." Conflict is resolved by adhering to the norm.

For 1.1, "After you, Alfonse. Whatever you say is OKAY by me." Conflict is avoided by not getting involved in the conflict argument.

For 9.9, "I'm not satisfied that we have the best answer. Let's go over it again until we are all committed to the same solution."

"Tom, why are you getting so emotional over this issue?"

Conflict is expected and respected. By testing, experimenting and searching for better facts, better solutions are uncovered. Also, by confronting the conflict itself and examining the relationship that exists among the group members, the group can break down the facades that cause the group members to hide from the truth.

Management Style Evaluation

When evaluating the management style of an individual, what does one look for? What element or elements of managerial orientation are significant and, once identified, what description of a specific orientation would help us define one of the five styles categorized on the grid as being different from the others?

This author was introduced to a system of style evaluation criteria when attending a management grid seminar in 1975. With the passing of time, and with each group meeting attended, every orientation element and its grid characteristic description now becomes more vivid, and is considered today to be of great value. For that reason, the system is recalled below:

Elements Of Managerial Orientation

Six managerial orientations were specified as being the most appropriate upon which to establish characteristic descriptions of the various management styles. They were as follows:

Element 1 - DECISIONS

Element 2 - CONVICTIONS

Element 3 - CONFLICT

Element 4 - EMOTIONS (TEMPER)

Element 5 - HUMOR

Element 6 - EFFORT

What characteristic statement about each of the above elements would now best describe a given management style? By investigating each element separately, the following style characteristics were then identified:

Element 1: DECISIONS

9.1 — I place high value on making decisions that stick.

1.9 — I place high value on maintaining good relations.

5.5 — I search for workable, even though not perfect, decisions.

1.1 — I accept decisions of others.

9.9 — I place high value on getting sound creative decisions that result in understanding and agreement.

Element 2: CONVICTIONS

9.1 — I stand up for my ideas, opinions and attitudes, even though it sometimes results in stepping on toes.

1.9 — I prefer to accept opinions, attitudes and ideas of others rather than to push my own.

5.5 — When ideas, opinions or attitudes different from my own appear, I initiate middle-ground positions.

1.1 — I go along with opinions, attitudes and ideas of others or avoid taking sides.

9.9 — I listen for and seek out ideas, opinions and attitudes different from my own.

Element 3: CONFLICT

9.1 — When conflict arises, I try to cut it off or to win my position.

1.9 — I try to avoid generating conflict, but when it does appear, I try to soothe feelings and keep people together.

5.5 — When conflict arises, I try to be fair but firm and to get an equitable solution.

1.1 — When conflict arises, I try to stay neutral or stay out of it.

9.9 — I have clear convictions, but respond to sound ideas by changing my mind. When conflict arises, I try to identify reasons for it and to resolve underlying causes.

Element 4: EMOTIONS (TEMPER)

9.1 — When things are not going right, I defend, resist or come back with counterarguments.

1.9 — Because of the disturbance that tensions can produce, I react in a warm and friendly way.

5.5 — Under tension, I feel unsure which way to turn or shift to avoid further pressure.

1.1 — By remaining neutral, I rarely get stirred up.

9.9 — I contain myself, though my impatience is visible.

Element 5: HUMOR

9.1 — My humor is hard hitting.

1.9 — My humor aims at maintaining friendly relations, or when strains do arise, it shifts attention away from the serious side.

5.5 — My humor sells myself or the position.

1.1 — My humor is seen by others as being rather pointless.

9.9 — My humor fits the situation and gives perspective. I

retain a sense of humor even under pressure.

Element 6: EFFORT

9.1 — I drive myself and others.

1.9 — I rarely lead, but extend help.

5.5 — I seek to maintain a good steady pace.

1.1 — I put out enough effort to get by.

9.9 — I exert vigorous effort and others join in.

Grid-Style Descriptions

Having identified style characteristics for each of the managerial orientations, it is now possible to regroup them to form *grid-style descriptions.* By selecting the appropriate paragraph, a grid-style identity is made possible. The reader may then identify a person by his or her management style. You may also "peg" yourself if you choose.

The following grid-style descriptive paragraphs are generated by regrouping the characteristics: (The reader is left the responsibility of assigning specific grid-style designations to the descriptions generated.)

A___ I accept decisions of others. I go along with opinions, attitudes and ideas of others and avoid taking sides. When conflict arises, I try to remain neutral. I rarely get stirred up. My humor is seen by others as rather pointless. I put out enough effort to get by.

B___ I place high value on maintaining good relations. I prefer to accept opinions, attitudes and ideas of others rather than to push my own. I try to avoid generating conflict, but when it does appear, I try to soothe feelings and to keep people together. Because of the disturbance that tensions can produce, I react in a warm and friendly way. My humor aims at maintaining friendly relations, or when strains do arise, it shifts attention away from the serious side. I rarely lead, but extend help.

C__ I search for workable, even though not perfect, decisions. When ideas, opinions or attitudes different from my own appear, I initiate middle ground positions. When conflict arises, I try to be fair but firm and to get an equitable solution. Under tension, I feel unsure which way to turn or shift to avoid further pressure. My humor sells myself or a position. I seek to maintain a good steady pace.

D__ I place high value on making decisions that stick. I stand up for my ideas, opinions and attitudes, even though it sometimes results in stepping on toes. When conflict arises, I try to cut it off or to win my position. When things are not going right, I defend, resist or come back with counterarguments. My humor is hard hitting. I drive myself and others.

E__ I place high value on getting sound creative decisions that result in understanding and agreement. I listen for and seek out ideas, opinions and attitudes different from my own. I have clear convictions, but respond to sound ideas by changing my mind. When conflict arises, I try to identify reasons for it and to resolve underlying causes. When aroused, I contain myself, though my impatience is visible. My humor fits the situation and gives perspective. I retain a sense of humor even under pressure. I exert vigorous effort and others join in.

A Primary and Back-Up Theory for Each of Us

As with EGO STATES and LIFE POSITIONS, we do not escape having our own management style. Not one, but two: a primary and a back-up style. And, to complicate matters even more, our style may change, depending upon the overall orientation of the group we happen to be functioning in, or as a result of the people we may be working with.

Based on our unique assumptions about life and other people, each of us has one of the five management grid styles as a primary style for ourselves while associated with one particular group.

We all seem to have a primary theory about how to manage, and if that doesn't work, then we fall back on our back-up style. Recognizing that each of us can operate primarily from any one of the five grid positions, the other four positions are then available to us as back-up positions.

Forces that Trigger the Back-Up Style

Forces which cause the back-up style to come into play are usually linked to the pressures of the situation: time pressure, frustration, certain types of people, difficult intellectual tasks, emotional stress, fatigue and boredom; all will cause the back-up style to be triggered.

— Fatigue will usually pull a person into the 9.1 style.

— Another variable is the importance of the problem. A problem of great significance pulls a person differently than one of trivia.

— Some people start in 9.1; plow through, bump into disagreement and, at that point, really pull back and begin to think in such a way as to explore the content of the mind of the other person who is in disagreement. This person is "backing" from 9.1 to 9.9.

— You can sometimes get beneath the 1.1 and lift the person up to where they were before they became a 1.1.

— Any style can become a back-up for any other style.

— The idea of *thickness* refers to depth of a style, i.e. the amount of agitation that must take place before a back-up style is triggered.

— At times, the primary style is so strong, it stays in effect even under pressure, fatigue, failure or disagreement.

— Alcohol can be a villain for peeling off the grid positions.

　1.　At 4:00 PM, two persons having worked on negotiations regarding a project, head for the local pub. Having worked long and hard on their negotiations, they commit themselves to mutual exploration, examining alternatives; (9.9). And, over the first cocktail, they continue to talk.

2. After a second drink, it was easier to shade differences; (5.5) and find a middle ground.

3. Another two drinks and it was decided they should worry about it tomorrow (1.9) since they owed it to themselves to relax after the hard day's work.

4. Back at the office, the other members of the organization know how the boss gets with a few too many. One or two more and his unreasonableness (9.1) arises.

5. It only takes one more, however, and it's off the grid the boss goes through the 1.1 exit.

Management Grid Training Seminars

Management grid seminars are conducted by many companies for their management, supervisory and hourly employees. Most management consulting firms, as well as schools of business having management development centers, would be capable of conducting such seminars for organizations. However, it would be more appropriate to have individuals within an organization participate with other persons who at first are unknown to each other. Old prejudices and biases would likely be less a factor than they would if members known to each other were to participate together in the same seminar.

A word of caution: management grid seminars can be stressful. The tactic normally employed over a period of several days is to get participants tired, hungry and irritable in order that groups have to function under conditions designed to trigger back-up styles. The human psyche is more elastic and definitely stronger than you might think, however, and what there is to be gained from such an encounter far out-weighs any name-calling that might take place among a few strangers who have an unbelievable and remarkable experience together.

CONCLUSION TO PART III

Part I of this book is devoted to the investigation of guest relations as they might be encountered from the guest's point of view, and as they might impinge on the individual service employee having to relate directly with that guest. Several philosophies relating to service were discussed, as were certain mores you might encounter if involved in the hospitality industry.

In Part II, Transactional Analysis (TA) and its many and varied spinoffs such as role playing, game playing, life positions, ego-grams and stroking are presented as tools to be used in interpreting "ego states" of guest and employees, both with which we must communicate.

In Part III, employee relations — those happenings and interrelationships that exist among management, supervisory personnel and front line workers — are presented as possibly having the greatest influence on a person's desires to treat our guest in a manner deserved. Specifically, employee relations are held as *"THE BASIS"* of quality guest relations.

Recognizing that the basic motivators of service personnel will be the prime cause of their wanting to give high quality, courteous and concerned service, aspects of various motivators are stressed. Classical theories are recalled. However, prime emphasis is placed on motivational environments and what seems to affect them in the most positive way.

A major point stressed is that workers have value. Seldom, however, do we as managers recognize the depth of this value until we learn to delegate properly and to rely on the decisions and actions of others. The commitment of each of our employees is based on our recognizing the value of our employees, then conveying to them our recognition of this value. When there is commitment, the employee becomes "turned on" and wants to be a part of something worthwhile.

Such an employee then begins to seek development, and to desire greater responsibility. To bring the morale of an employee to this point requires an understanding of how we as managers affect each employee through our management types, systems, and styles.

By management type, we find ourselves identified as either autocratic or democratic, benevolent or consultative, authoritative or participative. We find ourselves involved in management systems that have numbers ranging from 1 to 4 and, finally, we find ourselves caught up in a system of management styles that identifies us by how, and how well we can resolve daily management and business conflicts.

The management grid system of evaluating management styles can provide growing executives with a framework by which they can take a good look at themselves and their contemporaries.

In Appendix E, there is a questionnaire which relates to the grid style descriptions found on page 255 of Chapter 12. Answering this questionnaire can provide insight to your basic and back-up management styles. Of even greater importance, however, would be to have one of your employees and one of your contemporaries answer the same questionnaire *about you.* How different would the results be? Does one dare to find out?

In the final analysis, we need look carefully at where we are expending our energies. Do we use our energies to suppress others, to worry, to look for quick fixes or avoid getting involved? We would do well to determine how we do expend our energies, and imagine the growth and performance that could be generated if such energies were directed toward seeking better, more workable, reasonable, intuitive and sensible answers to our daily business challenges.

ENDNOTES

1. Henry L. Sisk; *Principles Of Management; A Systems Approach to the Management Process* (Cincinnati: South - Western Publishing Company, 1969), pp. 538-539.

2. R. R. Blake, J. S. Mouton, L. B. Barnes, L. E. Greiner, *Breakthrough in Organization Development,* Harvard Business Review, Vol. XXXXII (November-December, 1964), pp. 133-155.

3. For a complete description of the Managerial Grid, See: Robert R. Blake and Jane S. Mouton, *The Managerial Grid* (Houston: Gulf Publishing Company, 1964).

4. Henry L. Sisk; *op. cit.,* p. 539.

APPENDIX A

Job Descriptions and Responsibilities

for

Guest Relations Positions

Individual hotels and motels prepare job descriptions to fit many needs in the industry. Here are several job descriptions with hotel operations which are for persons having primary guest contact responsibilities. There are other areas for which job descriptions are prepared but guest contact may be limited.

The following job description is prepared for a front office clerk/receptionist as written by a large hotel chain:

JOB DESCRIPTION

Hotel/Motel Receptionist

Alternate job titles: Front desk clerk, guest service agent

Basic Function: Provide hospitality and service to guests, receive and register guests and assist guests with their needs and requests so that they will enjoy their stay, wish to return again and recommend the hotel to others.

Work Performed: Welcome and register guests, obtain proper guest identification and establish method of payment.

Take credit card information.

Time-stamp registration card. Obtain guest departure

date.

Sell up (act to sell higher-rate rooms). Suggest food and beverage services and other hotel services.

Record the number of room keys issued.

Prepare "due out" (list of departing guests) by 1:30 p.m.

Be prepared at all times to answer guests' questions and help solve their problems.

Post guest charges.

Process accounts of departing guests.

Verify all after-departure charges.

Reconcile all charges and cash received during the work shift and prepare the cash drop.

Keep front office neat and presentable at all times.

Prepare airline arrivals.

Pre-register new arrivals.

Process room charges as they are reported.

Verify the housekeeping report.

Prepare bed turndown report.

Prepare 6:00 p.m. house count.

Prepare separate list of VIPs and be certain they are given special welcome.

Job descriptions can be written to elaborate the details of the job. This one, for the job of hotel reservations manager, shows the percentage of total time typically devoted to the various tasks: about a quarter of the time being spent in taking reservations, about 20 percent used in assisting the room clerks and the rest of the time devoted to the other tasks listed.

JOB DESCRIPTION

Reservations Manager

Basic Function: Supervise and perform all reservation operation, along with related clerical duties. Direct programs geared to the special corporate high-volume reservation.

Work Performed:	**Percent of Time**
Process reservation information received through telephone, and personal contact with guests and potential users of our hotel.	25%
Type reservation confirmations for all individual, group convention guests.	15%
Acknowledge the receipt of reservation deposits to guests and coordinate with the accounting department.	2%
Work with the sales department on group room sales.	15%
Conduct weekday lunches for individuals responsible for booking reservations for their companies at area hotels.	3%
Prepare the following reports - Weekly Forecast, Weekly Reservation, and Monthly Reservations Statistics.	5%
Operate "Reservation II" - (incoming and outgoing messages system), all phases of operation.	5%
Assist room clerks with check-in of all groups, tours and conventions.	20%
Attend all hotel meetings.	10%

An indication of the concern being given to guest services in America is the introduction of the job of concierge. This job has existed in luxury European hotels for a long time. The European hotel concierge has been traditionally filled by men who work from a desk separated from the reception area. In this country, most major hotel chains such as Sheraton, Hyatt, Marriott, Stouffers and others have added concierges to provide additional service. The job is filled by both men and women. Some hotels have identified "floors" for concierge service.

Here are parts of the concierge job description as written by a leading hotel chain.

JOB DESCRIPTION

Concierge

Basic Function: Provide service to guests by expanding the abilities of the front office to give personalized service with few time restraints.

VIP Handling

Limousine schedule & maintenance.

Bud vase or bouquet ordering & set-up in room.

Greeting upon arrival (note in room if not feasible).

Expedite check-out if possible.

Daily call to the guest.

Amenity Items Requested for or by Guests - Arrange Billing

Flowers

Amenity book items

Special arrangements needed

Coordination with Group Leaders on Bulk Tours (10 + Persons)

Restaurants

Hotels

Civic events

Theatre

Car rental

Airlines

Sports

Lobby

Brochures

Flowers

Secretarial/Copy/Beeper Service, Guest Mail & Messages

Oversee concierge lounge on designated floors, tend the buffet table and keep the coffee hot and drinks cold.

Liaison with Social & Local Business

Other guest-contact jobs that may be unfamiliar to the reader include those of sales representative, convention manager, social director, maitre d'hotel, wine steward/stewardess. General descriptions of these jobs, taken from *Resources For Tourism/Hospitality/Recreation,* published by the Canadian Government Office of Tourism, Ottawa, are seen here:

Sales Representative, Hotel Services

Contacts representatives of government, business and social groups to solicit business for hotels or resorts. Selects prospective customers by reviewing information concerning functions such as sales meetings, conventions, training classes and routine travel by organization members. Calls on prospect, analyzes requirement of occasion, outlines types of service offered and quotes prices. Verifies reservations in person. Confers with customer and hotel department heads to plan function details such as space requirements, publicity, time schedule, food service and decoration. Serves as a convention adviser or hotel agent during functions to resolve problems, such as space adjustment and need for additional equipment.

Convention Manager

The major responsibility of the convention/banquet manager is to attract major conventions and business meetings to the hotel. To accomplish this requires some promotional and communication skills, and ability to manage sales personnel. The convention manager promotes the hotel facilities and services available, ensuring they meet the needs of the convention and meeting planners, and advises, coordinates and organizes to ensure the success of the particular event.

Social Director

Plans and organizes recreational activities and creates friendly atmosphere for guests in places such as hotels, resorts and aboard passenger ships. Greets new arrivals, introduces them to other guests and acquaints them with recreational facilities. Encourages guests to participate in group activities. Ascertains interests of group and evaluates available equipment and facilities to plan activities, such as: card parties, games, tournaments, dances, musicals and field trips. Arranges for activity requirements such as transportation, decoration, refreshments, entertainment and setting up equipment, and assists in resolving guests' complaints.

Maitre D'Hotel

Supervises and coordinates activities of workers engaged in serving patrons in formal dining room, and greets and escorts customers to tables. Inspects dining room and equipment for cleanliness and ensures that staff are well-groomed and correctly attired. Receives and records telephone reservations, greets guests at dining room entrance, verifies reservations and assigns tables. Escorts guests to tables and seats them. Speaks with guests at table to ensure satisfaction with food and service. Determines appropriate measures to settle valid complaints, such as adjusting bill, replacing meal or providing free liquor. Thanks guests upon their departure and provides courtesies such as aid with coats. Deposits money in safe at closing of dining room.

Wine Steward/Stewardess

Suggests and serves wine to guests in formal setting in hotels, restaurants and similar establishments. Studies menu and wine list to recommend wines complementary to food orders. Greets guests, presents wine list and suggests appropriate wines. Takes wine order and obtains wine from bartender. Adds wine cost to food bill. Drapes wine bottle in table napkin, places in appropriate holder or ice basket and carries to tables. Adjusts napkin to expose label of bottle so that guest may verify order. Opens wine bottle, pours small amount into glass for tasting by guest and fills other glasses when wine is approved. Checks frequently to refill glasses and to ensure that needs of guests are met. Instructs busboy/girl to replace wine glasses according to types of wine being served. Removes empty bottles and wine containers from table and replaces in storage area.

Executive Housekeeper

The Executive Housekeeper is in primary control of the cleanliness and servicing of guestrooms, and the general cleanliness of all public areas in the rooms portion of the hotel. Other titles seen for this position may be: Director of Services, Director of Internal Services or Director of Housekeeping

Operations. This position, although considered as servicing the "back of the house," is very much a guest-contact position. Additionally, all persons working under the executive house-keeper are expected to communicate with guests to make them feel welcome and wanted.

All persons filling the above jobs perform functions which cause them to engage in guest relations.

APPENDIX B

Review Questions

1. Which of these descriptions best fits the manner in which a desk clerk/receptionist should dress?

    a. conservatively

    b. informally

    c. comfortably

    d. appropriately for the clientele

2. What kind of role does the receptionist play?

    a. management representative

    b. problem-solver

    c. salesperson

    d. all of the above

3. The front office of a hotel can be considered:

    a. its focal point

    b. its nerve center

    c. its command post

    d. a crossroads, a juncture

    e. all of the above

4. Good techniques in answering the phone include:

    a. answer as soon as possible, ordinarily within three rings

b. greet the caller pleasantly; make him or her feel that you are pleased to receive the call

c. allow the caller to hang up first if possible

d. all of the above

5. To make telephone usage more efficient:

a. maintain a reference file of much-used numbers

b. plan what is to be said before calling

c. speak distinctly into the phone

d. all of the above

6. When placing a caller on "hold," it is courteous to:

a. return to the line every 30 seconds

b. return only when you have information

c. return to the line every two to three minutes

d. none of the above

7. When a person calls requesting the room number of a guest, the desk clerk should:

a. politely give the caller the number

b. connect the caller with the room but don't give out the number

c. refuse the request and hang up

d. none of the above

8. In case of overbooking:

a. be calm, be mature, apologize for the hotel

b. check to see if there are any "house use" rooms that could be rented

c. rooms that have been blocked out for airline personnel can be checked to see if they will be occupied

d. all of the above

9. Which one of the following phrases may be offensive to hotel guests?

    a. May I ask how long you plan to stay with us?

    b. Do you plan to pay by check or cash?

    c. That's against house policy for you to do that.

    d. May I suggest . . .

10. The _____ largely determines where lies that thin line between being friendly and over-familiar with the guest.

    a. class of clientele

    b. age of hotel

    c. geographic area

    d. season

    e. employee's personality

11. One of the best techniques for cooling any tense situation is to:

    a. make a positive show of strength and superiority

    b. have the person removed from the building

    c. speak loudly and with a firm voice

    d. speak slowly and calmly

    e. none of the above

12. Which of the following statements about "body language" is true?

    a. it varies from one culture to another

    b. much "body language" is a learned behavior

    c. many interpretations may be made concerning a single gesture or movement

    d. all of the above

13. How could a desk clerk improve the talking and listening aspect of hotel guest relations?

    a. by repeating for clarity when the guest says something important

    b. by looking at the speaker so that the speaker knows he or she has your undivided attention

    c. by pausing often in the conversation

    d. all of the above

14. In guest relations:

    a. look the guest in the eye

    b. smile with the eyes

    c. smile with the face

    d. all of the above

15. Which of these indicators best signifies a level of tension of the speaker?

    a. facial expressions

    b. the voice

    c. posture

    d. dilation of the pupils in the eyes

Discussion Questions

1. Come those times when a guest is downright rude, even belligerent and physical, perhaps no manager is available to take on the situation. Should you stand up for your rights and personal dignity even though you surmise doing so will arouse the guest even more?

2. As a female receptionist, how would you react to an obvious lewd joke told at your expense?

3. Is it possible for a desk clerk/receptionist to be too friendly on the job?

4. The subject of body language has been enthusiastically endorsed by many people. Is there danger that confidence in reading body language can be overdone?

5. The job of concierge is seen in many luxury European hotels. In what kinds of hotels would concierges be appropriate in this country? Would the job be adjunctive and helpful to the job of receptionist? Should the concierge report to the front office manager or directly to the general manager?

6. How long, if ever, do you think it will before 100-room hotels and motels are computerized?

7. Do you think some people are constitutionally equipped to become outstanding receptionists?

8. Is it important for receptionists in first-class hotels to hold at least an associate degree?

9. Suppose your hotel has a policy of not honoring a reservation if the guest arrives after 6:00 p.m. A guest comes in at 7:00 and explains that his plane was late. What should you as a receptionist do?

10. Suppose you work as a receptionist in a hotel whose clientele you despise as a group. Feeling as you do, is it possible to continue to act friendly and hospitable toward them?

APPENDIX C

Survey I

An Objective EGO-GRAM

Mark each statement with a (+) or (-) as it may or may not apply to you personally. Place the appropriate mark by each of the 75 statements. If you are uncertain or feeling "neutral" on a particular statement, pass on to the next statement. First impressions or thoughts are the best ones to record. Most people usually have positive feelings on about 30 to 35 of the statements.

1. I find it easy to comfort others when they are upset or worried.

2. Often there are occasions when I tell myself, "Be quiet, you're talking too much."

3. I enjoy driving fast, and I do it often regardless of speed limits.

4. I evaluate criticism before I react to it.

5. I tend to criticize others frequently.

6. I make a great effort to avoid hurting other people's feelings.

7. I make an effort not to exaggerate other people's strengths and weaknesses.

8. I am uncomfortable in an unstructured situation.

9. I demand perfection from myself.

10. I have a tendency to make impulsive purchases.

11. I think about the consequences of my actions before I act.

12. I find it easy to be sympathetic with other people's problems.

13. I have a tendency to be rebellious when I don't get my own way.

14. Most of our present problems have developed because our society is too permissive.

15. I often find myself being concerned with the approval of others.

16. I am an argumentative, domineering person.

17. I often daydream and fantasize.

18. I tend to keep my true feelings bottled up inside myself.

19. I can see no purpose in sensitivity or encounter group sessions.

20. I often find myself thinking, "I can't do this, I shouldn't do that, or I better not do that."

21. I like to wear brightly-colored clothes.

22. My behavior indicates that I really believe, "It is not whether you win or lose, but doing your best is what's important."

23. I have established realistic and meaningful goals for myself.

24. I tend to look for the good things in other people.

25. When I'm bored, I hide it from others.

26. I tend to express my anger when I get mad rather than hold it in.

27. I tend to agree with others rather than argue about what to do.

28. When I fail to meet my own expectations, I tend to

encourage myself to do better next time rather than to brood about my failure.

29. I find it easy to support others when things are going badly.

30. I tend to gather facts and plan carefully before starting some action.

31. There are certain fundamental truths about morals, right and wrong, and religion to which people should be more dedicated.

32. In a tense situation, I would tend either to withdraw or laugh to relieve the tension.

34. I am not reluctant to voice my opinions and back them up, but I respond to sound ideas by changing my mind.

35. People who know me would say that I am very critical of other people.

36. I often find myself telling other people not to worry.

37. I rarely challenge authority.

38. People seem to turn to me for advice and counsel.

39. I am very possessive of my personal belongings.

40. We need to devote more of our energy to respecting our laws instead of changing them.

41. I have no difficulty expressing my emotions in appropriate circumstances.

42. I tend to look on the bright side of situations.

43. I don't allow myself to cry in front of other people.

44. My feelings often cause me to act spontaneously without considering the consequences of my actions.

45. I am highly critical of myself.

46. "A little kindness goes a long way" is a philosophy that I not only believe in but also put into practice.

47. I have a well-developed set of rules and regulations for my personal behavior.

48. I seek out ideas, opinions, and attitudes different from my own.

49. When I get mad, I manage to keep a calm appearance, even though I may be churning inside.

50. I express my emotions freely — sometimes even inappropriately.

51. A woman's place is in the home.

52. I am able to retain control over my emotions in times of stress.

53. My friends would say that I am an uninhibited person.

54. I am very self-conscious.

55. It is easy for me to make myself feel better when I'm afraid or discouraged.

56. People who know me would say that I am very opinionated.

57. I am decisive, but no one is afraid to disagree with me.

58. I spend a lot of my time helping others and enjoy doing it.

59. I have a hard time expressing my emotions freely.

60. I often do things just for the pure fun of it.

61. I believe that there is a time and a place for everything.

62. I am open-minded rather than opinionated.

63. When someone needs sympathy or encouragement, I have no difficulty in providing it.

64. People who know me would say that I place a high value on humility and tactfulness.

65. I would cry openly at a good friend's funeral.

66. I make an effort to learn things for myself.

67. I tend to be self-centered.

68. I tend to help people who are having trouble rather than ignore them or make fun of them.

69. I have a set way of doing almost everything.

70. I spend a lot of my free time reading books.

71. I don't take many risks.

72. I tend to be rigid and firm rather than liberal in my philoso-phies and attitudes.

73. People who know me would say that I have a lot of fun.

74. I do not tend to be overcritical of myself.

75. I rarely let people know the real me.

SCORING KEY

DIRECTIONS:

The questions you have answered are divided into five categories. If your response to a question was (+), you receive one point in the appropriate category. Exceptions are questions #19 and #32 which require a (-) response to receive a point. Refer to your answer sheet and determine the number of points you scored in each of the five categories. (Circle all positive responses, and negative responses on #19 and #32 if necessary.)

NP	CP	A	FC	AC
1	5	4	3	2
6	9	7	10	8
12	14	11	13	15
22	16	19	17	18
24	20	23	21	25
28	31	30	26	27
29	35	34	32	33
36	40	38	39	37
42	45	41	44	43
46	47	48	50	49
55	51	52	53	54
58	56	57	60	59
63	61	62	65	64
68	69	66	67	71
74	72	70	73	75

Totals

Grand Total _____

PERCENTAGE CONVERSION TABLE
Individual Category Score

Total Score	1	2	3	4	5	6	7	8	9	10	11	12	13	14
20	5	10	15	20	25	30	35	40	45	-	-	-	-	-
21	5	10	14	19	24	28	33	38	43	-	-	-	-	-
22	4	9	14	18	23	27	32	36	41	-	-	-	-	-
23	4	9	13	17	22	26	30	35	39	-	-	-	-	-
24	4	8	12	17	21	25	29	33	38	-	-	-	-	-
25	4	8	12	16	20	24	28	32	36	-	-	-	-	-
26	4	8	12	15	19	23	27	31	35	-	-	-	-	-
27	4	7	11	15	18	22	26	30	33	37	41	-	-	-
28	3	7	11	14	18	21	25	29	32	36	39	43	-	-
29	3	7	10	14	17	21	24	28	31	34	38	41	-	-
30	3	7	10	13	17	20	23	27	30	33	37	40	-	-
31	3	6	10	13	16	19	22	26	29	32	35	39	42	-
32	3	6	9	12	16	19	22	25	28	31	34	38	41	-
33	3	6	9	12	15	18	21	24	27	30	33	36	39	-
34	3	6	9	12	15	18	20	24	26	29	32	35	38	-
35	3	6	9	11	14	17	20	23	26	29	31	34	37	-
36	3	6	8	11	14	17	19	22	25	28	31	33	36	-
37	3	5	8	11	14	16	19	22	24	27	30	32	35	-
38	3	5	8	10	13	16	18	21	24	26	29	31	34	37
39	3	5	8	10	12	15	18	20	23	26	28	31	33	36
40	2	5	8	10	12	15	18	20	22	25	28	30	32	35
41	2	5	7	10	12	15	17	20	22	24	27	29	32	34
42	2	5	7	10	12	14	17	19	21	24	26	29	31	33
43	2	5	7	9	12	14	16	19	21	23	25	27	30	33
44	2	4	7	9	11	14	16	18	20	23	25	27	30	32
45	2	4	7	9	11	13	16	18	20	22	24	27	30	32
46	2	4	6	9	11	13	17	15	20	22	24	26	28	30
47	2	4	6	8	11	13	15	17	20	22	24	26	28	30
48	2	4	6	8	10	12	14	17	19	21	23	25	27	29
49	2	4	6	8	10	12	14	16	18	20	22	24	26	29
50	2	4	5	8	12	12	14	16	18	20	22	24	26	28

EGO-STATE PROFILE

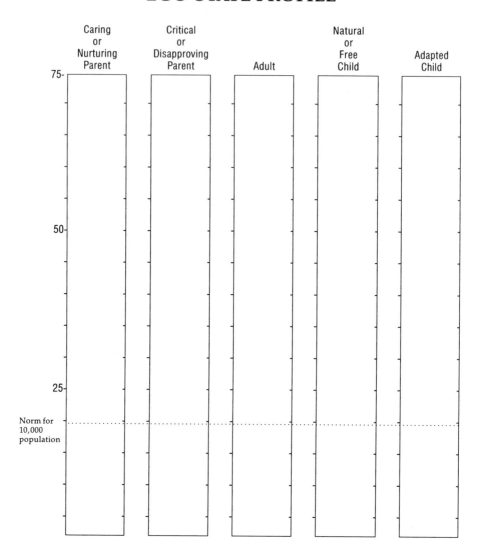

By transferring your scores in each of the five categories to the appropriate scales above, you will construct an EGO-GRAM. This is an ego-state profile which is an indication of how you expend your energy. It represents both the intensity and the frequency of activation of each of your ego states. In a population of 10,000 participants, the normal distribution occurred at 20% in each of the five EGO STATES.

APPENDIX D
Survey II
Leadership Questionnaire

Answer each of the 18 questions below with a definite "Yes" or "No".

Some questions you will be able to answer offhand, almost without thinking. A few will require careful thought. Be sure to answer ALL the questions and answer them as truthfully as you can, since you are the person who will benefit by knowing where your strong points are and where you have opportunities for improvement.

YES   NO

1. Do you enjoy "running the show"?

2. Generally, do you think it's worth the effort to explain the reasons for a decision or policy before putting it into effect?

3. Do you prefer the administrative end of your work — planning, records, and so on — to the actual supervision of people?

4. A stranger comes into your department; he was hired by one of your assistants. When you first approach him, would you first ask his name, then would you introduce yourself?

5. Do you keep your people up-to-date on all developments affecting the group?

6. Do you find, in giving out assignments, you tend to state the goals and leave the methods up to your subordinates?

YES   NO

7. Do you think that it's good common sense for a leader to keep aloof from his or her people because, in the long run, "familiarity breeds contempt"?

8. A date has to be decided for a group outing. You've heard the majority prefer Tuesday, but you're sure Thursday would be better for everyone. Would you put the question to a vote rather than make the decision yourself?

9. As a manager, do you see your role more as that of a planner and arranger as opposed to one who should direct and control an operation?

10. Do you find it fairly easy to fire someone?

11. Do you feel that the friendlier you are with your people, the better you'll be able to lead them?

12. After working on a particular problem for a considerable period of time, you finally work out the answer, but your assistant pokes your solution full of holes. Would you be annoyed that the problem is still unsolved, rather than become angry with your assistant?

13. Do you agree that one of the best ways to avoid problems of discipline is to provide adequate punishment for rule violations?

14. Your way of handling a situation is being criticized. Would you try to sell your viewpoint to your group, rather than make it clear that, as boss, your decisions are final?

YES   NO

15. Do you generally leave it up to your subordinates to contact you, as far as informal, day-to-day communications are concerned?

16. Do you feel that everyone in your group should have a certain amount of personal loyalty to you?

17. Do you favor the practice of appointing committees to settle a problem rather than stepping in to decide on it yourself?

18. Some experts say differences of opinion with a work group are healthy; others have a different view. They feel that this indicates basic flaws in group unity. Do you agree with the first view?

KEY

Consider only the YES answers.

If a majority of your answers to questions 1, 4, 7, 10, 13, or 16 were YES; your leadership style tends toward an "Authoritative" style.

If a majority of your answers to questions 2, 5, 8, 11, 14, or 17 were YES; your leadership style tends toward a "Consultative" style.

If a majority of your answers to questions 3, 6, 9, 12, 15, or 18 were YES; your leadership styles tends toward a "Participative" style.

APPENDIX E
Managerial Grid Style Descriptions

Consider all of the statements under Element 1 (i.e., A, B, C, D, E). Circle the one which best describes you. Follow the same procedure for Elements 2, 3, 4, 5, and 6. Transfer your answers to the scoring sheet.

Element 1: DECISIONS

A I place high value on making decisions that stick.

B I accept decisions of others.

C I place high value on maintaining good relations.

D I place high value on getting sound, creative decisions that result in understanding and agreement.

E I search for workable, even though not perfect, decisions.

Element 2: CONVICTIONS

A When ideas, opinions or attitudes different from my own appear, I initiate middle-ground positions.

B I listen for and seek out ideas, opinions and attitudes different from my own. I have clear convictions, but respond to sound ideas by changing my mind.

C I prefer to accept opinions, attitudes and ideas of others rather than push my own.

D I stand up for my ideas, opinions and attitudes, even though it sometimes results in stepping on toes.

E I go along with opinions, attitudes and ideas of others or avoid taking sides.

Element 3: CONFLICT

A When conflict arises, I try to identify reasons for it and to resolve underlying causes.

B When conflict arises, I try to cut it off or to win my position.

C I try to avoid generating conflict, but when it does appear, I try to soothe feelings and to keep people together.

D When conflict arises, I try to remain neutral or stay out of it.

E When conflict arises, I try to be fair but firm and to get an equitable solution.

Element 4: EMOTIONS (Temper)

A When things are not going right, I defend, resist or come back with counterarguments.

B Because of the disturbance tensions can produce, I react in a warm and friendly way.

C When aroused, I contain myself, though my impatience is visable.

D Under tension, I feel unsure which way to turn or shift to avoid further pressure.

E By remaining neutral, I rarely get stirred up.

Element 5: HUMOR

A My humor is seen by others as rather pointless.

B My humor sells myself or a position.

C My humor is hard-hitting.

D My humor aims as maintaining friendly relations or, when strains do arise, it shifts attention.

E My humor fits the situation and gives perspective; I retain a sense of humor under pressure.

Element 6: EFFORT

A I rarely lead, but extend help.

B I seek to maintain a good steady pace.

C I put out enough effort to get by.

D I exert vigorous effort and others join in.

E I drive myself and others.

CHARACTERISTIC EVALUATION

ELEMENTS		ANSWERS			
1.	A	B	C	D	E
2.	A	B	C	D	E
3.	A	B	C	D	E
4.	A	B	C	D	E
5.	A	B	C	D	E
6.	A	B	C	D	E

Primary .... (Greatest number of occurences)

Back-Up .... (Second greatest numbers of occurences)

For Results: Check against statements found on page

THIS IS AN EVALUATION OF _____

THIS IS A SELF-EVALUATION _____

INDEX